Thomas K. Johnson

Christian Ethics in Secular Cultures

World of Theology Series

Published by the Theological Commission of the World Evangelical Alliance

Volume 2

Thomas K. Johnson

Christian Ethics in Secular Cultures

WIPF & STOCK · Eugene, Oregon

Wipf and Stock Publishers
199 W 8th Ave, Suite 3
Eugene, OR 97401

Christian Ethics in Secular Cultures
By Johnson, Thomas K.
Copyright©2014 Verlag für Kultur und Wissenschaft
ISBN 13: 978-1-5326-5486-2
Publication date 4/2/2018
Previously published by Verlag für Kultur und Wissenschaft, 2014

Contents

Introduction

One of the most important questions in Christian ethics is the relationship between the moral principles we should follow before God within the Christian community and the ethics followed in the secular societies within which we live. This question became painful when I toured the preserved World War II Nazi concentration camp at Dachau as a teenager (August 1972). After the mental shock receded, I heard a statement by Corrie ten Boom which clarified the relation between the principles followed by the Nazis and those followed by Christians. She simply said, "They think differently than we do." At the very same time, it was clear to ten Boom both that many of the Nazis knew that their actions were wrong and that the actions of the people she represented can have a large influence on what happens in entire societies. That is our dilemma: 1. We claim we have received a revelation of God's moral will in the Bible and in creation which must shape the distinct identity of believers individually and in community over against unbelieving cultures; 2. We know our neighbors follow the ethics of other worldviews (such as the Nazis), which can easily wreak destruction in the lives of millions of people and entire societies. We have both a moral duty to a distinct, separate Christian identity in contrast with the cultures in which we live and a universal moral duty to love our many neighbors who are hurt because of the ethical principles flowing from other worldviews and religions. The millions who died in the Holocaust were my neighbors whom Jesus taught me to love. The millions of people who get hurt or killed because the ethics of some other religions do not promote freedom of religion are my neighbors whom Jesus taught me to love. The millions of people who get seriously hurt because the ethics flowing from their worldview does not support healthy family life are my neighbors whom Jesus taught me to love. How should we, as Christians whom God has called to a separate moral identity in the Body of Christ, participate in the moral considerations that shape the lives of people in entire cultures, knowing the role of other worldviews and religions in the ethics of those cultures, and really love our neighbors?

This dilemma helps us understand a theme that runs throughout the Bible. On the one hand, at least since the time Moses led the people of God out of Egypt during the Exodus, believers have had to take both practical and symbolic steps to maintain their distinct moral and spiritual identity as separate from the surrounding culture. The ancient Israelites were repeatedly warned to flee from the idolatry of their neighbors and all the immoral and inhumane practices that were associated with that idolatry. For example, in Leviticus 18:21 they were warned, "Do not give any of your children to be sacrificed to Molech, for you must profane the name of your God." God's people were called to a separate and distinct moral identity. And the continual, urgent need to maintain their distinct moral identity, in contrast with the surrounding nations, formed the background for important symbolic actions; good examples are the ritually cleansing of physical goods captured in war (Numbers 31:21-23) during the era of conquest and the way Daniel and his friends rejected the fine foods of Babylon during the era of captivity (Daniel 1:1-20). But on the other hand, believers were prophetically driven to address the immorality of the surrounding nations, especially when it reached the level of crimes against humanity. (See Amos 1 for a good example.) Believers were and are supposed to become morally sensitive people, and this means we are truly appalled at what happens to people, even when these atrocities follow from the ethics of other religions and worldviews.

It seems to me that this prophetic engagement of Old Testament believers with their world was partly in fulfillment of the promise given to Abraham. Not only would Abraham become a "father of many nations" (Genesis 17:5), emphasizing the distinct identity of the people of God, but God also gave a universal promise to Abraham, "All peoples on earth will be blessed through you." (Genesis 12:3) Already in the Old Testament there was a joint moral concern for the ethically distinctive identity of God's people and a universal concern for the principles that influenced the nations and all the people being hurt by those nations.

This two-sided moral concern is also evident in the New Testament. On the one hand, there is an abundance of evidence that the apostles were very concerned about the moral identity of new believers. For example, Paul wrote, "Do you not know that the wicked will not inherit the kingdom of God? Do not be deceived: Neither the sexually immoral nor idolaters nor male prostitutes nor homosexual offenders nor thieves nor the greedy nor drunkards nor slanderers nor swindlers will inherit the kingdom of God. And that is what some of you were." (1 Corinthians 6:9-11) We Christians are supposed to be truly different from the world around us. On the other hand, Jesus taught us, "You are the salt of the earth. ... You are the light of the world (Matthew 5: 13, 14), which leaves me with the unavoidable impression that believers are to take responsibility for what is happening in the world around us, which necessarily includes the moral principles shaping the world around us. It was no accident that the early church slowly began to reshape the Roman Empire.

The essays that follow were written while I lived and worked in the context of the secularism that is shaping the western, post-Christian world. For almost 20 years I taught ethics, philosophy, and religions in different secular universities in the US and Europe, and for several years I was the pastor of an evangelical church largely comprised of Christians who were students or staff in one of the most secular universities in the US. But these essays are not only relevant for western culture. Because of the globalization of the media and entertainment, secular western ideas about sexuality, family, and business assault the senses around the world. Letters I have received make me think that Christians from other continents can benefit from reading how western Christians are responding to the ethics of secularism.

The following chapters are in three groups of sections:

1. Questions of sex, marriage, and family

2. Questions of work and business

3. Theological and philosophical foundations.

It is my conviction that in one way Christian ethics must be purely biblical. That means that we truly follow the Bible as our authority, so that Christian ethics is the exposition of Scripture. On the other hand, as soon as we take up the second half of our moral dilemma, i.e., what is happening in societies around us, some of us need to speak like social scientists and philosophers. For this reason I will freely move from studying texts in the Bible to engaging in philosophical reasoning or making use of research in the social sciences. This is part of being in the world but not of the world.

SOLI DEO GLORIA

Chapter 1: What Makes Sex So Special?

The Question: What's So Different about Sex?

"Thou shalt not commit adultery." Exodus 20:14

"Why *shouldn't* sex be treated like any other activity? Why should we consider it moral to play tennis with somebody we don't love but immoral to have sex with somebody we don't love? Why should we consider it moral to eat lunch with somebody of the same sex but immoral to have sex with that same person? Why should we be permitted to go to a movie purely for pleasure but not have sex purely for pleasure? What's so different about sex that it requires such special rules?"[1]

To be fair to Olen and Barry, editors of the book in which this declaration occurs, we must notice that they are attempting to articulate the ideas embodied in the so-called Sexual Revolution of the late twentieth century. They may not fully agree with these ideas, but they have nicely summarized some very common opinions and questions of our time. People are asking, "Why should we think traditional sexual ethics are anything but arbitrary, irrational taboos?" Someone else will add, "Didn't modern contraception set us free from all this crazy nonsense about keeping sex within marriage?" A third voice might say, "If you think your God wants to keep sex inside marriage, it shows that your God is not very nice or has a bad sense of humor. Does your God just want to take all the fun out of life?"

Questions of this type are extremely important to many people, and important questions deserve honest, thoughtful answers. As a Christian I believe that our truly BIG questions are answered by the Bible. This means that in regard to understanding our sexuality, we should look for answers that are informed by the Bible. However, before jumping to answers, it may be wise to ask a counter-question – really a question about the questions. This counter-question should be as follows:

Observers of modern secularism point out that, because of secularization, people are often left with a reductively naturalistic interpretation and experience of life. The "naturalistic" part of this refers to thinking and talking as if all that really exists is that which is natural, material, or physical. The "reductive" part of this phrase refers to the way in which a naturalistic worldview tends to be reductive or to reduce our understanding of our own

---

[1] Jeffrey Olen and Vincent Barry, *Applying Ethics: A Text with Readings,* fourth edition, (Wadsworth Publishing Company, 1992), p. 72.

life experience. If all that exists is what is natural or physical, the only experiences one expects to have will be physical experiences. The Sexual Revolution was closely tied to the development of secularism.[2] The Sexual Revolution proclaimed sexual freedom; however, wasn't the real result quite different – a reduction of sex to an empty, shallow physical experience? The best support for this counter-question or critique of the Sexual Revolution comes from reading the writers and philosophers who were supporters of secularism and the Sexual Revolution.

One of the most articulate philosophical supporters of the Sexual Revolution was Alan H. Goldman, especially his article "Plain Sex."[3] Goldman pointedly rejects any "means-end analysis" of sex; that is, he rejects any understanding of sex that connects sexual activity to another purpose, whether "reproduction, the expression of love, simple communication or interpersonal awareness." To understand sex properly, he claims, it must be "plain sex" – without other associations. Sexual desire is nothing more than desire for contact with another person's body. Goldman thinks false views of sexual morality arise from the silly idea that sex is properly something more than physical contact, whether love, communication, or whatever.

I am not the only person who thinks Goldman put the wrong title on his essay. If sex is what he thought it is, a better title might be "Empty Sex" or "Sub-Human Sex." Because Goldman is a naturalist, his understanding and experience of life are dramatically reduced. He has a reductive understanding of sexuality, meaning his understanding and experience of sex is reduced to much less than sex was meant to be. His philosophy would support what many call sexual freedom, but the cost of this freedom is astonishingly high: the loss of everything human about sex. I find this price far too high. Might there really be something so different about sex that it requires special rules?

The secularist loss of an understanding of sexuality is also evident in the writings of Jean Paul Sartre.[4] He wrestled with how to create meaning in a meaningless world. According to Sartre, if God does not exist, there can be no "essence" of human life that comes before the "existence" of particular people. This means there is no proper pattern or scheme of life

---

[2]   This interpretation of secularism is dependent on Thomas C. Oden, *Two Worlds: Notes on the Death of Modernity in America & Russia* (Intervarsity Press, 1992).

[3]   Contained in Olen and Barry, pp. 86-97.

[4]   This interpretation of Jean Paul Sartre is dependent on C. Stephen Evans, *Existentialism: The Philosophy of Despair & the Quest for Hope* (Zondervan Publishing House, 1984.)

that people should follow or that gives meaning to life; we are forced to choose freely how we want to live. In the realm of sexuality, this means it is impossible to say that monogamy is better than polygamy, polyandry, or constantly changing relationships. We are condemned to freedom. However, this does not close the topic. In his novel *Nausea,* he shows that people use love and sex as a way of searching for meaning in life, though this effort is not always successful. For Sartre knows that love and sex can easily become meaningless, manipulative, or boring if meaning is not brought into the relationship.

The terminology of Sartre is entirely different from that of Goldman, reflecting different philosophical traditions. However, their overall perspectives are remarkably similar regarding sexuality. They agree that sexuality has no necessary meaning or distinctive content that would lead to particular moral rules governing sexual relationships. They also agree that there is no fixed pattern for responsible sexual activity, whether heterosexual monogamy, homosexuality, polygamy, or continuous fluctuation. In this way, they would both support the Sexual Revolution and reject any traditional Christian perspective on sexuality. I am left wondering if the quest for sexual freedom has cost us a large part of our humanness.

Recently I was moved to tears by a "reality show" on a German television station. Young unmarried couples with children were offered paternity tests to see if the mother's current partner was the biological father of the woman's child or children. A young mother was "sure" her current partner was the father, though she acknowledged it could possibly be either of two men, given the week of conception. On live television, the couple received the report from a genetics laboratory that her current partner was *not* the biological father.

The tears they shed were not just the result of the foolish choices of immature people. Their foolishness and immaturity were supported by a culture that says sex should be treated like any other activity, not much different from having lunch with someone. Their lives embodied a message we hear all around, in schools, in books, and in the media. Might we be ready to receive some wisdom from the past and from on high? Is there no better way?

The Answer: What *Is* So Different about Sex!

The Bible gives profound answers to the question of what is so different about sex that it requires special moral rules. I would explain those answers in these terms: Sex can best be described as an "interpersonal sacrament" which should properly occur within marriage, a "creation order," because there is a close correspondence between the meaning of the interpersonal sacrament and the creation order. The biblical commandments about sexuality are not arbitrary rules from a fun-hating deity; they are designed to protect our humanness. This perspective leads to a much richer understanding and experience of the closest human relationships. This is a very substantial alternative to the reductive naturalism that says that sex is only about physical contact. This alternative says that there is a created pattern or "essence" of human life, and following this pattern is one of the steps that gives us meaning in everyday life.

How is having sex with someone different from having lunch with that person? Briefly stated in other words, sex requires special rules because God created us in such a way that marriage and sex fit together in a particular way. This is what we see in the pages of the Bible and in everyday experience. A crucial biblical text is Genesis 2:15-25.

"The Lord God took the man and put him in the Garden of Eden to work it and take care of it. And the Lord God commanded the man, 'You are free to eat from any tree in the garden; but you must not eat from the tree of the knowledge of good and evil, for when you eat of it you will surely die.' The Lord God said, 'It is not good for the man to be alone. I will make a helper suitable for him.' Now the Lord God had formed out of the ground all the beasts of the field and all the birds of the air. He brought them to the man to see what he would name them; and whatever the man called each living creature, that was its name. So the man gave names to all the livestock, the birds of the air and all the beasts of the field. But for Adam no suitable helper was found. So the Lord God caused the man to fall into a deep sleep; and while he was sleeping, he took one of the man's ribs and closed up the place with flesh. Then the Lord God made a woman from the rib he had taken out of the man, and he brought her to the man. The man said,

'This is now bone of my bones and flesh of my flesh;
She shall be called "woman," for she was taken out of man.'

For this reason a man will leave his father and mother and be united to his wife, and they will become one flesh. The man and his wife were both naked, and they felt no shame." [5]

We are told in this text describing the origins of the human race that a man will "be *united* to his wife," or as our older translations read, "a man will *cleave* to his wife." The Hebrew word translated "cleave," "*dabaq*," is a very interesting way of describing the sexual embrace, for it brings to-

---

[5] Quotation from the New International Version.

gether two meanings of the same word. On the one hand, this word means to cling physically to something. This word is used when a person's tongue clings to the roof of his or her mouth (Psalm 137:6) or when a man's hand clings to his sword in battle (2 Samuel 23:10). On the other hand, this word is used to describe tight bonds of loyalty and affection. During a time of intense uncertainty and fear, King David's army was described as clinging to him (2 Samuel 20:2). Clearly, this word is describing deep, heartfelt commitments of loyalty and affection that endured through good and bad times.

In Genesis 2, it is not immediately obvious if this word refers to Adam and Eve physically clinging to each other or emotionally bonding to each other. Nevertheless, this is not a question that needs a simple either/or answer, especially if, as I think, we are reading sacramental language. In relation to God, we should understand a sacrament to be a symbolic action instituted by God that serves as a sign and seal of the covenant of grace between God and His people. A sacrament confirms both His grace to us and our faithful loyalty to Him. Sacramental language has a distinctive feature; because of the close association between the symbolic action and the meaning of the symbol, the *names* of the action and the *meaning* of the action are freely mixed and transferred. In the Old Testament, the term "circumcision" could refer either to the symbolic action or to the covenant relation symbolized by this action. Something similar happens in the New Testament regarding Holy Communion and Baptism. (Standard biblical examples are Genesis 17:10; Matthew 26:28; and Titus 3:5.)[6]

When Adam and Eve were clinging to each other, this was *not* a sign and seal of their relationship with God. However, on a human, interpersonal level, it was a sacramental action signing and sealing a covenantal bond. Their "clinging" to each other was both the sexual embrace and the bonded relationship symbolized and confirmed by the sexual embrace. In this sense, Protestants have historically called sexual intercourse a "holy sacrament" of the covenant of marriage.[7] Stated differently, more psychologically, sexual intercourse communicates much of the marriage covenant and vow nonverbally and symbolically. Because of the way we were created, sex is one of our strongest forms of nonverbal communication; sex is a promise of affection and loyalty, not only to each other but also to the children who may result from the relationship. The physical union is a sign of

---

[6]   See also Westminster Confession of Faith, chapter 27, for the way this theme was taught in historic Reformation theology.

[7]   Herman Bavinck, *The Philosophy of Revelation* (Longmans, Green, and Co., 1909; Baker Book House, 1979), p. 276.

a more comprehensive union, including spiritual, emotional, and social aspects of life. This is what makes sex so different from casually having lunch or coffee with someone. Sex communicates promises of a very significant nature, whether or not the couple is aware of it. It is foolish to try to separate sex from the process of bonding inside a marriage or from the children who may be conceived through that bonding.

If sex is a sacrament of marriage, obviously one must ask, "What is marriage?" Is it merely a worthless document from a useless government office? Our answer to this question today can easily be prejudiced by our tendency to think that only physical objects can truly be real. Since marriage is not a physical object that one can touch, some tend to think it is not real or a real thing. Without thinking, a person may be comparing marriage to something like a coffee cup, a window, or a streetlight. This is a serious mistake that influences how we act. Moreover, unfortunately, our English translation of the commandment "you shall not commit adultery" does not immediately correct this mistake. However, the Dutch (*niet echtbreken*) and German (*nicht ehebrechen*) translations are a little better, since both of these Bible translations refer to not breaking a marriage. This way of talking has a significant advantage, since it says more clearly that a marriage is something real that can be broken, though obviously the way in which a marriage can be broken is quite different from how one breaks a cup or a window.

So what is marriage, this thing we must be careful not to break? One of the best descriptions is a "creation order." This means it is a relational structure given by God in creating us that serves our good as well as God's various purposes. This way of describing marriage invites a comparison with other God-given structures we call creation orders, such important realities as work, government, and worship, through which God organizes our lives. It also means that marriage is not exactly something that we create; it is something that already exists, with some defined rules and boundaries, before we ever enter into it.

The term "creation order" tends to lead us to view marriage somewhat from the outside, as a social structure. We should also emphasize that marriage is a lifetime covenant between a man and a woman, and this covenant is publicly declared so everyone can know that a particular man and a particular woman stand in this lifetime covenant.[8] This is the internal content

---

[8]   A covenant is both similar to and different from a contract. A contract is usually very specific, well-defined, and limited in scope, such as a contract to rent an apartment or do a particular job. In contrast, a covenant may not be so well-defined, since we simply cannot know what may come our way in a lifetime. On

of marriage: a man and a woman solemnly covenant to become life partners. Those who think marriage is just a piece of paper have confused one part of the public declaration of the marriage (the legal part) with the covenantal reality that is being publicly declared. In the original creation, the only thing that was not good was that Adam was alone. God corrected this deficiency by creating Eve and by creating marriage. Marriage is a creation order with a lifetime covenant as its internal content; sex is an interpersonal sacrament that confirms and communicates this covenant in a nonverbal way.

Though it may be hard for us to think this way, marriage truly is something real, even though it is not a physical object. In addition, it has some enduring characteristics that we cannot change; it is monogamous, heterosexual, exclusive, and it lasts a lifetime. It can be compared to the law of gravity, which is also very real, though we cannot see it directly. However, the likelihood of people getting hurt by ignoring the reality of marriage is much greater than the likelihood of getting hurt by trying to ignore the law of gravity. Most of us just accept the law of gravity, whereas some try to ignore the reality of marriage.

Once we grasp something of the close connection between sex and marriage, it makes sense to ask about the purposes of sex and marriage together. This really should be one question, rather than separating the purpose of sex from the purpose of marriage. Of course, many people think of the purpose of sex as being pleasure, emotional release, or bonding, while they see the purpose of marriage as primarily in the realm of financial/legal questions. This separates matters that more properly belong together.

One of the first purposes of marriage is companionship. Adam, Eve, and most of the rest of us find it is simply not good to spend our lives alone. Most of us need a life partner. Our work, our toys, and our pets are simply not enough. Companionship is the primary thing we should both seek and seek to preserve in marriage.[9] Closely tied to this is one of the purposes of sex, that of total-person bonding. We read that Adam and Eve

---

the other hand, a covenant is also unlimited, since it involves one's total life, not something as limited as committing to a job or apartment.

[9]   We must be careful not to think that marriage (or sex) will provide total meaning or salvation, thereby solving all our problems. As an atheist, Sartre recognized that sex and marriage do not provide meaning; meaning must be consciously brought to the relationship. Christians should say even more clearly than did Sartre that sex and marriage do not provide meaning; they have meaning if received as a way in which we can glorify and enjoy God in gratitude.

were naked but not ashamed. Their comfortable physical intimacy contributed to a very wide-ranging unity of their lives.

People today are quite aware that sex can be very pleasurable. What needs to be added to that is an understanding that the pleasure of sex is different from other types of pleasure. Some pleasures can be enjoyed almost as much alone as with other people. This is obviously very different from normal sex. Other pleasurable activities, such as a sporting event, a concert, or a movie, are normally shared with other people. Nevertheless, in most of these pleasures, the people with whom we share the pleasure are all together relating to something else, the sport, music, or film, which gives them the shared experience. Our attention, emotionally and mentally, is focused on the sport, music, or whatever brings us together. However, sex is different in the important sense that it is the other person who gives pleasure, not some other entity or event. Our attention is totally focused on the other person. Sex is much more clearly an interpersonal event or experience than are our other normal forms of pleasure. The pleasure, sometimes intense, could be seen as a gift of God specially added to the companionship, a distinct type of pleasure that helps confirm and strengthen the covenantal ties between a husband and wife.

In the wisdom of God, the context in which children should normally come into the world is this context of bonded, loyal companionship and love. The companionship that men and women need forms the right situation for children to get a start in life. We should not hesitate to say that childbearing/child rearing is one of the purposes of marriage and sex. This is not to say that a childless marriage is not a proper marriage. And this is also not to say that sex always has to be intended to lead to pregnancy or even to be open to pregnancy. Nevertheless, it is very unwise for us to separate sex, marriage, and childbearing. There are natural connections among marriage, sex, and childbearing in the biblical descriptions of people and in our lives today.

As I write these words, I am riding on a train from Berlin, Germany, where I was lecturing in our seminary, to Prague, Czech Republic, where I live. Seated three or four rows behind me is a group of young German men who have been into their beer since mid-morning. If I understand their drunken songs and slurred speech correctly, they are headed to Prague to enjoy the strip show discos and "sex professionals." While listening to them, I have been reminded of the wry comment in Proverbs 6:26, "The prostitute reduces you to a loaf of bread." Very likely, these men will have some interesting sexual experiences this weekend. But they probably have not thought much about what they are missing or how they are being treated (or the probability that the prostitutes are being held as slaves by highly organized criminals). They are missing the experiences that help bond a man and woman into lifetime partners, and the habits they are developing will make it more difficult for them to experience such satisfying bonding in the future. Very likely, they do not appreciate the way the prostitutes reduce them to something as exchangeable and disposable as a piece of bread; nor that hiring a prostitute is dehumanizing in a way that it is not dehumanizing to hire a taxi driver or a dentist.

The ancient words written in stone, "You shall not commit adultery," do not call us to a joyless, boring existence. By giving us a firm "No" and some unchanging rules, God calls us to a richer, higher, more human type of life. Why can't we acknowledge that sex is different from other activities – different in a way that requires special rules?

Chapter II: Sex, Marriage, and Science

Since the time of the Enlightenment, religiously based ethics have had a bad reputation among many western intellectuals. Sigmund Freud could be taken as a spokesman for many scholars and educators in the way he saw Judeo-Christian ethics as irrational, guilt-producing, and falsely restrictive of natural freedom. Along with many others, Freud wanted a more "rational" approach to ethics. And if this rejection of religiously based ethics has had a central point of conflict, it could easily be in rejecting Judeo-Christian ethics with regard to marriage and sex, a rejection that came to cultural prominence with the "sexual revolution" of a generation ago. It is probably less common that secular intellectuals have explicitly rejected Judeo-Christian moral standards with regard to murder, theft, or lying. Now this rejection of religiously based ethics is being called in question from a direction that may be surprising to some: empirical research in the social sciences. Numerous recent empirical studies in psychology and sociology have shown that people generally experience a much higher level of well-being and happiness if they practice life-time marriage and keep sexual relations within marriage. There is no longer any reason to see traditional religious rules against divorce and extra-marital sex as the irrational impositions of an arbitrary or non-existent God. Scientific research shows that the traditional religious rules about divorce and extra-marital sex are so deeply rooted in human nature that a reasonable person will affirm and follow them, whether or not one believes in God. Thus, this same social science tends to support the claim that these rules are God-given and built into creation.

Before looking at the social science it is good to recall what has been normally claimed by Christian ethicists. The claim is not only that moral rules come from God; the claim is also that proper moral rules tend to contribute to the human good because these rules are rooted in or correspond to human nature and relationships. This is true whether one is talking about the ethics of sex, truth telling, protecting life and property, or other spheres of life. Outside of biblically informed ethics there is a strong tendency to separate matters of duty (deontological ethics) from matters that contribute to human well-being (utilitarian ethics). This secular tendency is often seen in popular discussions that separate religious duty from human happiness. But within the biblical perspective, there is no separation of considerations of God-given duty from considerations of human well-being. In the Bible there seems to be no tension between saying one should follow a moral rule because it comes from God and saying one should follow a moral rule because it contributes to the human good. For example, after receiving The Commandments from God and giving them to the people, Moses could use the language of duty before God to explain the importance of keeping the rules. "God has come to test you, so that the fear of God will be with you to keep you from sinning" (Exodus 20:20). On the other hand, Moses could also use moral language that sounds teleological, that ties moral rules to the human good, when he explains why people should follow the rules. "Walk in all the way that the Lord your God has commanded you, so that you may live and prosper and prolong your days in the land that you will possess." (Deuteronomy 5:33) The two are perfectly united because God is the source of moral duty and principles of human well-being.

An ethicist who understood this especially well was Princeton theologian Charles Hodge. He saw a complete unity of moral rules commanded by God and principles that serve the human good because "there is an imperfect revelation of [God's] law in the very constitution of our nature."[10] Many biblical laws are "founded on the permanent relations of men in their present state of existence," or, as he sometimes says, "are founded on the nature of things; that is, upon the constitution which God has seen fit to ordain."[11] With this in mind we can turn to the social sciences.

A social scientist who is very highly regarded for his ability to synthesize the results of social research by hundreds of social scientists from around the world is David G. Myers. In his various books he seems to take pleasure from using the results of research in the social sciences to destroy the myths that everyone supposedly "knows." In this study we will use Myer's compilation of research results in the social sciences. Myers invites this type of use of his works, for he openly acknowledges his deep Christian faith, and he has written some interesting studies on the relation between religion and psychology.[12] But Myers writes as an academic psy-

---

[10] Charles Hodge, *Systematic Theology,* Vol. 3 (Grand Rapids: Wm. B. Eerdmans, reprint 1986; originally published in the 1870s), p. 267.

[11] *Ibid.*

[12] Some of his studies on the relationship between psychology and the Christian faith include: David G. Myers, *The Human Puzzle: Psychological Research and Christian Belief* (New York: Harper & Row, 1978); *The Inflated Self: Human Illusions and the Biblical Call to Hope* (New York: Seabury, 1980); T. E. Ludwing, M. Westphal, R. J. Klay, & D. G. Myers, *Inflation, Poortalk, and the Gospel* (Valley Forge: Judson Press, 1981; M. Bolt & D. G. Myers, *The Human Connection: How People Change People* (Downer's Grove: InterVarsity, 1984); and D. G. Myers & M. Jeeves, *Psychology Through the Eyes of Faith* (San Francisco: Harper & Row, 1987, 2002).

chologist who is both an award winning researcher in his specialty of social psychology and the author of textbooks that are some of the most widely read in Western culture.[13]

His approach to psychology is that it should be based on precise research, not on speculation, ideology or anecdotes. He says,

> My vocation, as one who distills psychological science for various audiences, is to pull together the emerging research and reflect on its human significance. ... I rely much less on compelling stories than on research findings. As an experimental social psychologist—one who studies how people view, affect and relate to one another—I'm not much persuaded by anecdotes, testimonials or inspirational pronouncements. When forming opinions about the social world, I tell people, beware of those who tell heart rending but atypical stories.[14]

To this he adds, "This scientific perspective is quite unlike the postmodern subjectivism that dismisses evidence as hardly more than collected biases."[15]

This does not mean that Myers believes that research and writing in the social sciences is somehow objective or unaffected by the worldview, bias or ideology of the social scientist. He openly confesses, "In looking for evidence, and in deciding what findings to report and how to report them, we are sometimes subtly steered by our hunches, our wishes, our values within."[16] However, Myers is confident that social scientific research performed according to exacting scientific standards and which is fairly reported can do much to overcome and correct personal hunches, popular wisdom and ideological pseudo-social science, all of which he regards as often being largely wrong.[17]

---

[13]   Some of Myers' widely used textbooks include *Psychology* (Worth Publishers, 6th edition), *Exploring Psychology* (Worth Publishers, 5th edition), *Social Psychology* (McGraw-Hill, 7th edition), and *Exploring Social Psychology* (McGraw-Hill, 2nd edition).

[14]   David G. Myers, *The American Paradox: Spiritual Hunger in an Age of Plenty*, Forward by Martin E. Marty (New Haven and London: Yale University Press, 2000), p. xiii. Though the title of this book is American, Myers often uses European research and address problems common to the entire Western world. His book could almost be called *The Western Paradox.*

[15]   *Ibid.*

[16]   *Ibid.,* p. xiv.

[17]   As one example, Myers often criticizes pseudo-scientific belief in the occult or in paranormal abilities, such as ESP, mental telepathy or mind reading. He writes, "Poke at claims of the occult and the paranormal, and time and again one is left

What Myers discovers in his extensive research in the social sciences is that human life and communities flourish and do well when people follow certain principles and develop the related patterns of behavior. And conversely, the opposite patterns of behavior are very destructive of human happiness and well-being. These results are so conclusive, Myers believes, that they should shape our definition of what it means to make responsible choices and decisions, whether in government policy, educational priorities, personal lifestyle choices or assessing what it means for the media to be socially responsible.

Many of the most destructive patterns of behavior in the developed world of the new millennium are closely tied to our rather extreme individualism. Myers summarizes radical individualism in these terms:

> Do your own thing. Seek your own bliss. Challenge authority. If it feels good, do it. Shun conformity. Don't force your values on others. Assert your personal rights (to own guns, sell pornography, do business free of regulations). Protect your privacy. Cut taxes and raise executive pay (personal income takes priority over the common good). To love others, first love yourself. Listen to your own heart. Prefer solo spirituality to communal religion. Be self-sufficient. Expect others likewise to believe in themselves and to make it on their own. Such sentiments define the heart of economic and social individualism, which finds its peak expression in modern America.[18]

Myers claims, on the basis of impressive amounts of empirical scientific research, not just his personal preference, that "for today's radical individualism, we pay a price: a social recession that imperils children, corrodes civility and diminishes happiness. When individualism is taken to an extreme, individuals become its ironic casualties."[19] For this reason Myers advocates, "a new American dream—one that renews our social ecology with values and policies that balance 'me thinking' with 'we thinking.' "[20]

An important part of the transition from a moderate individualism to an extreme or radical individualism, Myers claims, was the so-called "sexual revolution" of the late twentieth century. And Myers is one of the many

---

holding a popped balloon. The more I learn about the human senses, the more convinced I am that what is truly extraordinary is not extrasensory perception, claims for which inevitably dissolve upon investigations, but rather our very ordinary moment-to-moment sensory experiences of organizing formless neural impulses into colorful sights and meaningful sounds." *Ibid.,* p. 265.

[18]   *Ibid,* p. 7.
[19]   *Ibid.* pp. 7, 8.
[20]   *Ibid.* p. 8.

sociologists who think the sexual revolution came at the cost of a terrible amount of human suffering. In regard to what he calls the "myth" that people should live together, cohabit, before getting married to see if they are compatible, he writes,

> Alas, the myth crumbles. Most cohabitations break up before marriage. In 1995, only 10 percent of 15-to 44-year-old women reported that their first cohabitation was still intact. But what about those who, after a trial marriage, decide to marry? Ten recent studies concur that couples who cohabit with their spouses-to-be have *higher* divorce rates than those who don't. Several studies illustrate:
>
> - A U.S. survey of 13,000 adults found that couples who lived together before marriage were one-third more likely to separate or divorce within a decade.
> - Another national study has followed 1,180 persons since 1980. By 1992, divorces had occurred among 29 percent of those who had co-habited before marriage and 13 percent of those who had not. In the 1995 National Survey of Family Growth, the corresponding divorce percentages were 26 and 15 within five years of marriage.
> - A 1990 Gallup survey of still-married Americans also found that 40 percent of those who had cohabited before marrying, but only 21 percent of those who had not, said they might divorce.
> - A Canadian national survey of 5,300 women found that those who co-habited were 54 percent more likely to divorce within 15 years.
> - A Swedish study of 4,300 women found cohabitation linked with an 80 percent greater risk of divorce.
> - And if either partner was a "serial cohabitor"—having previously co-habited with one or more others besides the spouse—the likelihood of divorce is even greater.[21]

Before looking at the effects of cohabitation on human well-being and happiness because of its association with divorce, Myers summarizes what has been learned by recent studies in psychology, sociology and economics that directly assess the effects of cohabitation.

> Women, especially, have paid a price for replacing marriage with cohabitation. Over their lifetimes, women have tended to work and earn less. Thus they have more to lose by replacing a legal partnership with a no-strings attached relationship. Upon separation or death, cohabitees have limited rights to each other's accumulated assets. The cohabitation revolution has therefore

---

[21] *Ibid.* p. 29.

not supported women's quest for economic parity with men. Perhaps due to their relative youth, lesser education, greater poverty and the presence of stepchildren, female cohabitees are also much more likely than married women to be victims of domestic violence. In Canada, they are four times more likely to be assaulted by their partner and eight times more likely to be murdered. In the United States, even after controlling for education, race, age and gender, people who live together are 1.8 times more likely than married people to have violent arguments.[22]

And to that summary Myers adds the further comment, "Cohabiting people are unhappier and more vulnerable to depression—an effect partly attributed to cohabitation's insecurity."[23] And though cohabiting couples tend to be at least as sexually active as married couples their age, yet those cohabiting are "less likely to report that their sex is physically or emotionally satisfying."[24]

Myers sees cohabitation as reducing human wellbeing because it replaces marriage for those currently cohabiting, tends to end in divorce for those who cohabit before marriage and also leads to reduced levels of happiness in marriage for those who cohabited before marriage.[25] The proper context for understanding this is provided by the tremendous amount of research in the social sciences that documents a very strong connection between marriage and a sense of happiness or well-being.

> Whether young or old, male or female, rich or poor, people in stable, loving relationships do enjoy greater well-being. Survey after survey of many tens of thousands of Europeans and Americans have produced this consistent result: Compared to the single or widowed, and especially compared to those divorced or separated, married people report being happier and more satisfied with life. In the United States, for example, fewer than 25 percent of unmarried adults but nearly 40 percent of married adults report being "very happy." Despite TV images of a pleasure-filled single life, and caustic comments about the "bondage," "chains," and "yoke" of marriage, a stubborn truth remains: Most people are happier attached than unattached.[26]

---

[22] *Ibid.* p. 30.

[23] *Ibid.* p. 32.

[24] *Ibid.*

[25] David G. Myers, *The Pursuit of Happiness: Discovering the Pathway to Fulfillment, Well-being, and Enduring Personal Joy* (New York: Avon Books, 1992), p. 163.

[26] *The Pursuit of Happiness*, p. 156.

In addition Myers points out, "People who say their marriage is satisfying ... rarely report being unhappy, discontented with life or depressed."[27] And "happiness with marriage predicts overall happiness much better than does satisfaction with jobs, finances or community."[28] However, "cohabitants are only slightly happier than single people."[29]

So what does divorce do to people? Myers agrees with many social scientists in his observation that divorce is very damaging to physical health. He quotes biologist Harold Morowitz, "Being divorced and a nonsmoker is slightly less dangerous than smoking a pack or more a day and staying married."[30] And Myers is quite aware of the way divorce tends to lead to emotional depression and economic poverty.[31] But Myers chooses to emphasize the effect of divorce on the children whose parents divorce, and in that discussion to also discuss the distinctive problems of children whose parents never get married.

One of the distinctive problems of children whose parents divorce or never marry is a much higher risk of suffering abuse at home. Myers reports, "A U.S. government study in 1996 found that children of single parents are 80 percent more at risk for abuse or neglect. A recent Canadian study of 2,447 allegedly abused children found that the proportion living in single-parent families was triple the proportion of two-parent families."[32] This leads Myers to affirm the U.N. Secretary General's claim that "family breakdown is reflected in ... child-abuse and neglect."[33] In addition Myers points out that, "Although usually caring and supportive, stepfathers and live-in boyfriends more often abuse children than do biological fathers, for whom selfless fatherly love comes more naturally." He also notes, "the incest taboo is weaker between stepfathers and stepdaughters they did not know as infants," and, "infants living with stepparents are at least 60 times more likely to be murdered (nearly always by a stepfather) than those living with natural parents."[34] Myers thinks the moral implication is clear:

---

[27] *Ibid.*

[28] *The American Paradox,* p. 43.

[29] *Ibid.* p. 43.

[30] *Ibid.* p. 43. Harold Morowitz is quoted in James L. Lynch, *The Broken Heart: The Medical Consequences of Loneliness* (New York: Basic, 1977), pp. 45, 46.

[31] *Ibid.* pp. 43 and 47.

[32] *Ibid.* p. 63.

[33] *Ibid.* p. 64. Myers is quoting from the Report of the Secretary General to the Forty-Eighth Session of the United Nations, Item 110, "Social Development Including Questions Relating to the World Social Situation, and to Youth, Aging, Disabled Persons, and the Family," August 19, 1993, p. 38.

[34] *Ibid.* p. 64.

"there can hardly be a better child abuse prevention program than the renewal of marriage."[35]

Another distinctive problem of children whose parents divorce or never marry is poverty. "Poverty claims 13 percent of children under age 6 living with two parents and nearly *five* times as many—59 percent—of children living with single mothers."[36] And Myers notes that the poverty rate is even higher among mothers who were never married.

A third distinctive problem is that of crime and delinquency among boys who grow up without their father in the home. Myers notes that "father-absence rates predict crime,"[37] and cites David Lykken's analysis that "the sons of single parents are at seven times greater risk of incarceration than sons reared by two biological parents."[38] Myers agrees with other social scientists in noting 70 percent as an almost magic number. Seventy percent of runaways, adolescent murderers and long-term prisoners come from fatherless homes. He notes that father involvement restrains male hypermasculinity and aggression, affirming Daniel Moynihan's analogy of an "invasion of barbarians," "teenage boys who become enemies of civilization unless tamed by father care and their entry into marriage and the provider role."[39] Myers is convinced that the "invasion of barbarians" within the developed countries is largely caused by the lack of fathers in the home during the boys' teenage years. This is generally either the result of divorce or the result of the parents never marrying.

A fourth problem that Myers notes among children whose parents divorce or never marry is a broad package of health, educational and psychological problems. Relating to psychological health Myers notes that "children of all forms of single-parent and stepparent families were two to three times as likely to have needed or received psychological help during the previous year."[40] And he adds, "even after controlling for sex, race, verbal ability and parental education, youths from nondisrupted families were half as likely to have been treated for psychological problems."[41] These problems are clearly not only an American phenomenon, for "One Swedish study of the more than 15,000 children born in Stockholm in 1953 and still

---

[35]   *Ibid.* p. 65.
[36]   *Ibid.* p. 73.
[37]   *Ibid.* p. 116.
[38]   *Ibid.* p. 117. The quotation is from David T. Lykken, "On the Causes of Crime and Violence: A Reply to Aber and Rappaport," *Applied and Preventive Psychology* 3 (1994): pp. 55-58.
[39]   *Ibid.* p. 77.
[40]   *Ibid.* p. 78.
[41]   *Ibid.* p. 79.

living there in 1963 found that 'parental separation or divorce has negative effects on later mental health whenever it occurs and regardless of the socioeconomic status of the household.'"[42] Myers thinks reports of this type are under-publicized.

On the issue of the physical health of children whose parents divorce, he notes, "Children from divided families are much more likely to engage in unprotected sex, smoke cigarettes and abuse drugs and alcohol." The total effect of divorce on children's health is such that "parental divorce predicts a shorter life by four years."[43] "Greedy morticians, it has been said, should advocate divorce."[44]

Children whose parents divorce or never marry also face increased educational and academic problems. "An analysis of Census Bureau data from 115,000 15- to 24-year-olds revealed that among whites, adolescent dropout rates were 61 percent higher among those in female-headed households."[45] Another study concluded, "the adjusted risk of dropping out of high school was 29 percent among children of lone parents or stepfamilies but only 13 percent among children of two-parent households."[46] And a different research group discovered that "children in intact families were, no matter what their age or race, half as vulnerable to school problems and were a third less likely to repeat a grade."[47]

On the basis of this research in the social sciences Myers affirms and advocates what he calls "the transcultural ideal: children thrive best when raised by two parents who are enduringly committed to each other and to their child's welfare."[48] Though this is not exactly the language of theology or philosophy, Myers is claiming that the best research in the social sciences shows that people find happiness and well-being when they follow the norms about marriage and family that the Judeo-Christian tradition considers to be God-given. This is a social science oriented type of natural law theory coming from a Protestant Christian who is one of the great social scientists of our time. Though Myers does not interact at length with theological or philosophical theories of natural law ethics, he does make an occasional passing comment on the topic. One of these makes the tie between

---

[42] *Ibid.* p. 82. Myers is quoting Duncan W. G. Timms, *Family Structure in Child-hood and Mental Health in Adolescence* (Stockholm: Department of Sociology, University of Stockholm, 1991), p. 93.

[43] *Ibid.* p. 79.

[44] *Ibid.* p. 80.

[45] *Ibid.*

[46] *Ibid.* p. 82.

[47] *Ibid.*

[48] *Ibid.* p. 87.

his social science and a Protestant version of natural law quite explicit. "Despite differing beliefs, faith traditions share many values. In *The Aboli-tion of Man*, C. S. Lewis in 1947 identified the morality—the seeming 'natural law'—shared by the world's cultural and religious traditions."[49]

What Myers calls "transcultural ideals" discovered by the social sci-ences are what theologians have called the natural moral law, the some-times unrecognized but always present God-given demand that we practice justice, love, faithfulness, honesty, etc.[50] Myers' work supports our claim that while philosophy can be relativistic, life is not relativistic, since there truly are norms that are present in human experience. Myers has investi-gated matters related to the need for practicing faithfulness in the realm of sex, marriage and family. Presumably other studies in the social sciences could show the need for following "transcultural ideals" in other realms of life. One could expect studies in economics to show the need for honesty, while studies in political science might show the need to practice justice.

The social sciences may not be able to prove that there is a natural mor-al law that is known and present in human experience because it comes to us from God through creation. But the social sciences can explain the claim and show at least some of the reasons why people should practice faithful-ness, honesty, justice, etc. This fits nicely with the historic Protestant claim that the natural law is closely associated with the civil use of the law. And in the civil use of the moral law, the important matter is that people do what is required by the moral law, whatever their motives and regardless of whether they understand what this law is and where it comes from.

Studies such as those compiled by Myers also show the need for recon-ciliation, forgiveness and healing in relationships between people and with God. This process of showing human need should be seen as closely relat-ed to the theological use of the law, which shows our need for grace. The

---

[49]   *Ibid.* p. 242.

[50]   Myers advocates an understanding of the relationship between psychology and theology that he calls "levels-of-understanding," which means that different aca-demic disciplines could describe the same phenomenon in somewhat different terms because the different disciplines examine the phenomenon at different lev-els. One could also say that different academic disciplines use methods suitable to understand different dimensions of reality. A "transcultural ideal" would be a so-cial science description of what theology calls natural law. See Myers' article "A Levels-of-Explanation View" in E. L. Johnson and S. L. Jones, editors, *Psycholo-gy & Christianity: Four Views* (Downer's Grove, IL: Intervarsity Press, 2000). The article in this volume by Jones and Johnson, "A History of Christians in Psy-chology," includes a concise summary of the type of model represented by Myers.

various uses of the moral law can never be totally separated, whether the law comes through creation or special revelation.

Chapter III: Foundational Values for Family Life and Public Policy[51]

It is a dangerous situation when a philosopher meddles in such practical affairs as government policy and child development. I remember Socrates' experience when he asked some foundational questions of his fellow citizens so many centuries ago; I hope I do not have to watch my wine glass with special care after this lecture. But it is my impression that the Athenians' frustrations with Socrates were not entirely with his quest for values; those frustrations arose partly because he mostly asked questions but did not always offer good answers. I will try to ask some questions and also offer some answers; obviously you are free to try to find better answers if you cannot accept my proposals. I am not afraid of disagreement, but please hold the Hemlock.

As a young man I had the privilege of being an academic assistant to the very significant social scientist David G. Myers. His wide-ranging, award-winning research in psychology and sociology was informed by a search for values and principles which would make human life flourish, a kind of Socratic quest. He dared to hope we can identify trans-cultural values which will promote human well-being, happiness, and the common good, and this hope led to his intensive research and extensive writing. He also claimed that it is the big things that have a big effect on human well-being, matters like key ideas and values, whereas he was convinced that many passing fads had relatively little influence on human well-being, no matter how aroused people may become in discussing different government policies and different styles of parenting. So in the spirit of Myers, I will suggest that ideas and values which we can bring into the formulation of policies, programs, and practices in the family, business, and government are more important than many particular decisions which we have to make. Those values and ideas will shape all our policies, programs, reactions, and relationships. Let me illustrate.

I. Children—Gifts or Problems?

At the beginning of all our thinking about children stands a fundamental philosophical question: what is this child? We can make the question more

---

51 This essay was originally a speech given at a conference for people shaping European government family policy in Prague, 2007.

pointed by asking, is a child primarily a gift or primarily a problem? Several years ago a pregnant colleague complained that her medical doctor saw her pregnancy as an illness, a problem, whereas she did not see the pregnancy as an illness or a problem. She saw the child as a great gift. The contrast in basic philosophy of life was stark. Forgive me for speaking plainly, but this contrast, nicely articulated in a medical clinic, is foundational for many matters related to children and child-rearing today. It is close to the low birth rates causing the declining population in many developed countries, close to how we treat mothers, close to how we treat each child, and central for policies in business and government.

This is a fundamental existential question that cannot be answered by a study in sociology or economics. Our answer will not only shape our policies and our treatment of each child; the future of western civilization depends on our answer. If we think children are most fundamentally problems to be avoided, we can avoid the problem and bring all of western civilization to an end. And without having clarified and discussed the question, this is the answer implied by our low birth rates in so much of the developed world. In contrast, I see my three children as three of the greatest gifts my wife and I ever received.

I would emphasize that our feelings toward children are an existential decision; by this way of talking I mean it may be impossible to prove to the satisfaction of all people that children are a gift. This is a decision that stands before and influences all our other decisions. A person could choose to see only the problems related to having children, e.g. medical problems, financial problems, loss of time and freedom, worries about their well-being. Babies are dirty, noisy, and expensive. But we can also choose to see the way in which our lives are so deeply enriched by having children, and also desire to pass on the gift of life to another generation. Such a choice is axiomatic in the sense that it comes before and informs rational and scientifically informed decisions. To say it is existential is to say it comes before rationality, provides the basis for rationality, and therefore might not be rationally demonstrable. In a deep sense, it is foundational for all of life, in families, in business, and in the wider culture.

If we decide to value children as gifts, not primarily as problems, this will lead to child-friendly policies in government and business; it will also change our personal reactions to each pregnancy, birth, and child. For example: do we rejoice when a colleague announces her pregnancy, or do we silently complain at the little problems that it will cause for our work? Which we do is determined by our prior value decisions; do we mostly look at the little problems, or do we decide to look at the way in which our lives can be enriched at every level (including the economic level) by the presence of another human being? Our value decisions may appear to be very hidden and private, but that is not really true. All of our actions arise from our value decisions, and in that manner our basic values are communicated.

I would also suggest that the children in our families, businesses, and communities will know from a very young age whether we see them as problems or gifts. Long before children can speak, they know many things at a deep, intuitive level that shapes their experience of the world. If they know that they are welcomed as gifts, they can more easily respond to life with basic trust, love, and the courage to become good citizens and neighbors; if they are seen as problems, their deepest anxieties are unduly aroused, leading to alienation from society and themselves. This is the path of delinquency, whether this alienation is expressed in drugs, crime, or gangs. Our private value decisions have a life-shaping effect on the children in our families, businesses, and wider community; our deepest feelings toward children set a deep direction to their response to their experience of life.

II. Loyalty Promotes Security

Long before they can express their thoughts in language, children seem to be aware of key elements in the value structure of their environment. This goes beyond the question of whether they are seen as gifts or as problems. It includes the presence or absence of interpersonal loyalty. The problem we need to consider is how to prevent children from having undue anxiety that they will be abandoned, especially abandoned by their parents. Anxiety about possible abandonment, or the experience of real abandonment, can easily cause a fundamental break in a child's relationship to society and to the world at large. Abandonment, or anxiety about abandonment, often undermines a child's basic trust and courage to exist. This is, I am convinced, the background to the very dismal statistics we have all read, about how the children of divorced parents have so many psychological, sociological, medical, and educational problems. These children feel abandoned by the people closest to them, and that experience has damaged part of their basic trust and courage. That is why, I think, that the statistics are so much worse when a woman bears a child as the result of a short relationship and never marries the father; that child was truly abandoned by the father from a very early age. Children as well as adults have a fundamental need for human loyalty. When this loyalty is broken, there is often damage to the spirit of

the person, damage which is expressed physically, socially, psychologically, or educationally.

Many times we find the school or state social agencies trying to solve
problems in the lives of children that arise because the children were perceived as problems and then felt abandoned by their mother or father. Of
course, we need to do all we can to help such people, but we also need to
ask about the value structure that will reduce the problem in the future. Part
of that value structure is lifetime marriage and family loyalty. Children
tend to flourish, with a stronger sense of basic trust and courage to exist,
when there is both real and perceived family loyalty; this family loyalty is
most often broken by divorce or separation. The divorce or separation of
parents very commonly leaves children feeling abandoned, which damages
their fundamental courage to live and basic trust toward life. And tragical-
ly, the majority of divorces seem to occur after relatively low levels of conflict, levels of conflict which could easily have been overcome or even forgotten.

Without resorting to totalitarianism, there is little a state can do to very
quickly eliminate the vast majority of divorces and separations; however,
the state can attempt to adopt policies and promote educational materials
that will communicate the message that interpersonal loyalty is a fundamental human need. Extreme individualism does not promote happiness;
loyalty and lifetime companionship promote happiness and empower our
children to flourish. This simple philosophical principle needs to be included in our schools, policies, and laws. It is a fundamental and humane value
decision that must be made, implemented, and communicated in the family, in business, and in state agencies. Once this value decision is made and
implemented, it can seem to become a self-authenticating and life-giving
part of the culture. After implementation of a wise value decision in public
policy, that policy or law tends to promote the genuine acceptance of the
basic value by the population, even if there is some popular frustration with
the policy at first.

III. Unconditional Love and Moral Structure

One of the most difficult challenges with regard to children has to do with
the relationship between unconditional love and the need for moral structure. On the one hand, we should all be aware of the way in which children
(and probably all people) have a deep need for unconditional love, or as
some phrase it, unconditional positive regard. The experience of such positive regard unleashes something powerful and creative within a person. In
a certain sense, it sets people free. Such positive regard speaks to our deep

need for acceptance by others. On the other hand, at the same time, children need practical moral guidance and restraint; they need clear, everyday rules regarding how to act and what not to do. And such practical moral guidance inevitably seems to imply that children (and people in general) are not acceptable if they do follow the rules, and that everyone fails at times.

This leads to a profound complexity at the level of basic values which we hold toward children and which we must communicate to children. Our children are simultaneously gifts which we unconditionally accept (and such loving acceptance has to be communicated) and also recipients of all the rigorous demands of responsible life in society (and these rigorous demands need to be effectively communicated) which are necessary to fulfill in order to be responsible people and good citizens. And such existential complexity has to be effectively communicated in the family, the school, and the society.

In philosophical terms, this is the problem of love and justice, which is also the problem of freedom and form; in the religious tradition it is frequently called the problem of grace and law or law and gospel. I am pretty sure I cannot solve the problem at the theoretical level; maybe no mortal can give a good explanation. I am also pretty sure that some type of dialectical interaction between the two principles is extremely important for our value stance toward children and for the moral content of our relationship to them.

Children have to hear and feel that they are deeply and unconditionally loved by their parents, by their school teachers, and by other authority figures in their lives, while at the same time they also hear and feel that life is filled with profound demands, some of which we might never completely fulfill. It is almost unavoidable that each person will be unbalanced in this question; some people will easily express unconditional love toward children, whereas others will easily express the demand for discipline and control. And society itself tends to fluctuate between these two poles. True authenticity is reached only at the point of fully embodying and communicating both love and justice, both form and freedom, completely at the same time. But who has reached such a level of personal maturity?

While we may never be able, whether theoretically or practically, to fully express unconditional positive regard (love) and also the need for deep moral discipline (rules, responsibility, and justice), we must take some steps in this direction. At this point, I am mostly forced to draw on my own experience as a parent of three responsible children. We have to consciously take steps to communicate both that we love our children and that life itself (not really us personally) imposes the need for moral discipline. We will need to tell them that certain behaviors are wrong, but we then should also tell them that we love them. We will need to stop our children from doing some actions, but that should be accompanied by our acts of affection, perhaps a hug or an embrace. On occasion children may need to be mildly punished for things they have done, but they also have to hear about our forgiveness when they apologize. And in this process, parents and teachers have to be extremely careful on several matters.

If children are only given unconditional love, without demands and discipline, they can easily become very happy with themselves but irresponsible toward others and toward society, a result none of us here wants. On the other hand, if children only receive discipline, rules, and demands, without much love and tenderness, they easily become bitter and angry toward life, again a result we want to avoid. If children have the feeling that rules and discipline are only the personal demands of a parent or teacher and not somehow the demands of life itself, they will be inclined to look for an opportunity to escape their restraints. And similar to the way in which unduly restrictive civil laws push people into crime, unduly harsh or restrictive discipline in the family or school can prompt rebellion. If children learn responsible behavior with a very small amount of external pressure or enforcement, there is a higher probability that they will internalize responsible behavior and the cognitive value structure that supports such behavior. Children (and probably adults, too) need a living combination of unconditional positive regard joined with sensible (not arbitrary) structure or discipline that fits the demands of life in society.

Comments

There are many detailed questions about child-rearing which resist once for all time, permanent answers. Each child has slightly different needs and opportunities, which have to be assessed by the parents to the best of their abilities. The role of the state is probably to remind parents of this responsibility and to provide advice and testing to assist parents in this responsibility. And many other matters that can seem very important for a short time may have a very small impact on the total lives of our children. They should be seen as matters in which we constantly look for ways to make small improvements, but these improvements should be recognized as small. Here I am thinking about things like the exact schedule of childcare and school, who organizes and pays for their care at what age, exactly how their medical care is organized, how much or which sports at which age, and a thousand other detailed questions. The big things are the big things, and among the truly big things are the ideas and values which we bring into the biggest challenge facing us as individuals and as western society: How do we train the next generation to become people of whom we can be proud and who will be grateful to us, as parents, educators, and citizens, for what they have received from us?

Chapter IV: Sabbath, Work, and the Quest for Meaning

"There is but one truly serious philosophical problem, and that is suicide. Judging whether life is or is not worth living amounts to answering the fundamental question of philosophy. ... I therefore conclude that the meaning of life is the most urgent of questions." Albert Camus (1913—1960) in "The Myth of Sisyphus."[52]

"Six days you shall labor and do all your work, but the seventh day is a Sabbath to the Lord your God." The Fourth Commandment in the Decalogue, Exodus 20:9-10.

When Camus penned these probing words about the meaning of life, he was speaking on behalf of many people in our time. That is probably why he won the Nobel Prize for Literature in 1957. His words interpret the experience of many: "Rising, streetcar, four hours in the office or factory, meal, streetcar, four hours of work, meal, sleep, and Monday, Tuesday, Wednesday, Thursday, Friday, Saturday--according to the same rhythm— this path is easily followed most of the time. But one day the 'why' arises."

For Camus, who was an atheist when he wrote these words, both the problem of meaning in life and the solution arose out of "absurdity," the unexplainable contrast between our daily free choices and desire for significance and a world that seems to be an endless, impersonal, uncaring chain of causes and effects that has no interest in our human struggles. According to Camus, there can be no fixed or given meaning to life if God does not exist. His solution, in the words of a character from one of his novels, is to try to become "a saint without God," that is, to live humanely, as a protest against blind, impersonal nature.[53] In this way, one can create meaning. Camus' hero is Sisyphus from classical mythology, who was condemned to spend his life pushing a rock up a large hill, only to have it roll down again. But rather than being miserable, Camus thought Sisyphus could be happy, and if I understand Camus correctly, Sisyphus could be happy precisely at the point when he glanced back at the stone rolling down the hill.

---

[52] This essay by Camus can be found in many good anthologies of texts in philosophy.

[53] The character is Tarrou from Camus' novel *The Plague* (New York: Modern Library, 1948), 229.

In response to Camus and our other neighbors who have many similar "why" questions, it is proper for us to turn to the biblical book of *Ecclesiastes* and say that though it sometimes seems that "all is meaningless" (*Eccl.* 1:2), yet meaning is found in relation to God (*Eccl.* 12:13). It is also good for us to respond to our neighbor's questions about meaning with the powerful words of the *Westminster Catechism* (Q. 1.), "Man's chief and highest end is to glorify God, and fully to enjoy him forever." In addition, we should use the Fourth Commandment in the Decalogue to address the question of meaning and purpose in life, "Six days you shall labor, and do all your work, but the seventh day is a Sabbath to the LORD your God" (Ex 20:9-10). On a weekly level we can and should experience meaning in the transition back and forth between worship and the work of the other six days.

The Sabbath commandment is God's call for us to recognize very practically that he has the right to structure our time--six ordinary days and one holy day. The Sabbath commandment is also God's call to recognize that he is the one who establishes the *meaning* of our time. Like Camus, many of our neighbors think they have to decide or create the meaning of life. In the Sabbath commandment God tells us both the meaning of our lives and how we experience that meaning. But Camus may have had an extremely helpful observation, that meaning or happiness may come in "looking back." This is what I would call the transition between Sabbath and ordinary days.

When God created Adam and Eve he said, "Be fruitful and increase in number; fill the earth and subdue it. Rule over the fish of the sea and the birds of the air and over every living creature that moves on the ground." (*Genesis* 1: 28) Christians have often called this verse the "cultural mandate," though we could also call it the "developmental mandate." God's purpose was that Adam, Eve, and their children would become sub-creators by working God's good creation. They were to develop families, farms, and communities, and all the learning and organization needed to make families, farms, and communities possible. All of this social, cultural, and economic development would have the glory of God as its center and focus. Worshipping and glorifying God was supposed to be the meaning and purpose of all that people do, in work and family, in society and culture.

The fall into sin distorted and disrupted everything. Instead of wanting to honor God, our first parents wanted to become like God (*Genesis* 3:5), which may mean to get rid of God or replace God. This new motivation then spread to all that people do in work, family, and culture. This new, sinful motivation came to prominent expression at the Tower of Babel (*Genesis* 11), which was an attempt to build a whole new culture and society, including all its families, farms, businesses, education, and organizations, without God. All these elements of culture and society were to find meaning and motivation in worshipping humanity in place of God. This sounds surprisingly like late modernity.

When God rescued his people from slavery in Egypt, he once again called them to work in his good creation as his sub-creators. "Six days you shall labor." However, unlike Babel, all the work of developing families, businesses, and communities was intended to lead to the Sabbath--the public worship of God. The six (not five or seven) ordinary days were to be a constant reminder that God created us and our world. After six days of diligence, the week was supposed to culminate and reach its climax in the Sabbath, by worshipping God in public community. The Sabbath was intended to give meaning and direction to the work of the six days. Honoring the Creator was intended to be the motivational center of all the effort, planning, and creativity needed to develop farms, families, businesses, and communities. In the Old Testament, the meaning of life is found in the transition between work and worship, between holy days and ordinary days. Diligent work makes a proper Sabbath possible, and Sabbath worship gives meaning and direction to the activity of the week's work. The Old Testament would teach us that we should work, in the family, business, or community, with a view to worshipping God, and we should worship God with a view toward working for God. Work leads up to worship, and worship gives purpose to work. In this way our lives will be filled with the proper meaning, doing all for the glory of God.

With the coming of the New Testament, the meaning of the Sabbath has been further enriched. God chose to raise his Son from the grave on Sunday--the first day of the week; therefore Luke seems to speak for the whole first generation of Christians when he said, "On the first day of the week we came together to break bread." (*Acts* 20:7) The Sabbath had been transformed into the "Lord's Day." In this transformation, our Lord took along the central meaning of the Old Testament Sabbath and added to it a celebration of his resurrection. For us, each Sunday is not only a Sabbath, but also a miniature Easter. Each week we are to celebrate not only the goodness of creation, we are also to rejoice in the resurrection and redemption. This enriched meaning of the Sabbath also enriches the meaning of the ordinary days of the week. The work of the normal six days finds its basis in both creation and redemption.[54]

The story of the Bible begins in the Garden of Eden (*Genesis* 2 and 3) and ends in the Holy City (*Revelation* 21 and 22). This makes it look as though the cultural or developmental mandate that God gave to Adam and Eve will remain in force into eternity. Our eternal hope is probably not to sit on a cloud and play a harp; in eternity we should expect to finally fulfill God's purposes in creating humans--that of being an entire society doing everything in every sector and dimension of life for the glory of God. When we fully receive all the benefits of Christ's resurrection in eternity, benefits that will transform our bodies, souls, and society, we will be able to engage in all the activities of the Holy City as fully restored people, fully human in every way God intends.

Every Lord's Day is a celebration of Jesus' resurrection; therefore, it is also a celebration of the coming Holy City that he will bring by the power of his resurrection. As the meaning of the Sabbath is enriched by the New Testament, so also is the meaning of the other days of the week enriched. We believers should see ourselves as the citizens of the coming City of God. Every Lord's Day is God's reminder and promise of who we will be in eternity. This promise, which stands at the beginning of the week, should shape the meaning of the rest of the week. Unlike Sisyphus, we are not doomed for eternity to roll a stone up a hill, only to have it roll down again. Whether in the home or in business, in school or in the community, we are citizens of the City of God, practicing and preparing for the real life to come. Part of the meaning of our lives today is to point forward to the coming eternal city, and we do this by the way we participate in the full range of normal activities on Monday through Saturday. So far as we can, we should think, talk, and act like citizens of the coming Holy City of God.

Camus used the ancient myth of Sisyphus to question the meaning of six days of ceaseless toil every week. Strangely, in that essay and in the retelling of the myth, Camus explicitly mentions every day of the week except Sunday. As an atheist, he could not understand Sunday nor see that Sunday is the clue to the meaning of the other six days. And yet, Camus noticed that meaning is found at the point of "looking back," the transition from one phase of life to another. The Fourth Commandment suggests that

---

[54] The way some cultures and nations have made Sunday the last day of the week reflects a loss of the sense of newness which Christians celebrate by making the day of resurrection our primary day of worship. The way in which entertainment has become the primary weekend activity shows that entertainment can easily become a worship substitute as part of the unavoidable quest for meaning.

the right transition to provide the experience of meaning is the continuous transition between work and worship. This Sabbath lets us not only worship God in gratitude for the goodness of creation, it also reminds us that the purpose of the ordinary days of the week is to glorify him at home and work, in school and society. This Lord's Day let us not only celebrate Christ's resurrection and the resurrection he has promised to us, it also give us pause to consider how to live and talk differently because we are citizens of the coming City of God. The transition between Sabbath and work is the answer to the meaning of life--one of the great problems of our time. The combination of hope, gratitude, joy, and purpose can drive every thought of meaninglessness and suicide from our minds.

Chapter V: The Spirit of the Protestant Work Ethic and the World Economic Crisis[55]

The world economic crisis has been painful. A Czech economist compares the pain with a hangover after a night of hard partying, implying that our developed economies have been drinking irresponsibly, that the changes needed are much deeper than merely taking some aspirin or buying a better brand of vodka.[56] Hardly any of us has been spared; many have experienced real financial pressure while observing devastation in the lives of others. Despairing thoughts have surely arisen in many hearts. We can be grateful that not so many in the developed world have been driven to suicide by economic angst; I am worried that the results will be worse for the many millions in the developing world or in economies that were already dysfunctional.

The very fact that I was asked to give this special lecture confirms my claim that we need to think deeply about the moral/cultural convictions that guide the economic dimension of our lives. We call this the study of "Economic Culture," which has especially interested Reformed Christians since Max Weber's fascinating study *The Protestant Ethic and the Spirit of Capitalism* a little over a century ago.[57] This topic interests us today because we need to learn from our past for our future.

Weber asked why parts of western civilization developed distinctive patterns that are not found in other cultures and civilizations. There is, he thought, a certain "spirit," meaning a distinctive definition of rationality,

---

[55] The following is a revised text of a public policy lecture given on behalf of the synod of the Evangelical Reformed Church of Lithuania, celebrating the 500th anniversary of the birth of John Calvin. The lecture was given on June 20, 2009, in Vilnius, Lithuania.

[56] The image comes from the blog of the Czech economist Tomaš Sedlaček: http://blog.aktualne.centrum.cz/blogy/tomas-sedlacek.php.

[57] Max Weber's study was originally published as an essay entitled *Die protestantische Ethik und der Geist des Kapitalismus* in 1904 and 1905 in volumes XX and XXI of the *Archiv für Sozialwissenschaft und Sozialpolitik*. It was republished in 1920 in German as the first part of Weber's series *Gesammelte Aufsätze zur Religionssoziologie*. It was published in English as *The Protestant Ethic and the Spirit of Capitalism*, translated by Talcott Parsons, with a foreword by R. H. Tawney (New York, Scribner, 1958; reprint New York, Dover, 2003).

that is seen in modern northern Europe which has led to a distinctively capitalist approach to work and business.[58]

According to Weber, greed, even unlimited greed, is not distinctive of capitalism and is neither the cause of capitalism nor caused by capitalism. People have always been greedy. What is distinctive of modern capitalism is the pursuit of profit, especially ever-renewed profit, by means of continuous, rational enterprise. Distinctively modern capitalism has three external characteristics: 1. Rational industrial organization (which means not pursuing merely speculative opportunities in the manner of capitalist adventurers). 2. The separation of business from the household. 3. The use of rational bookkeeping. But these external characteristics alone will not explain modern capitalism; modern capitalism is also characterized by an internal ethic that says people can find *meaning* through their work. Systems of meaning, claimed Weber, are usually religious in source, even if particular people may have forgotten the religious roots of their system of meaning. Even people who are not consciously religious often continue to live, think, react, and emote in ways they regard as "rational" or "natural," even though these "natural" or "rational" ways are historically rooted in distinctive religious traditions not shared by the rest of the world's population. Authentic modern capitalism has an internal ethic that says people find meaning in part through self-denial (worldly asceticism) in their work.[59] This modern capitalist work ethic is, Weber claimed, the result of the Calvinist work ethic, carried on in a secularized manner. He called it "The Spirit of Capitalism."

As an example of the Calvinist work ethic, the spirit of capitalism, Weber selected Benjamin Franklin. Religiously Franklin was a deist, not a Calvinist, but Franklin illustrates the way in which a religiously rooted cultural value system can come to full fruition among people who do not accept the religious beliefs of a previous generation. For Franklin, time is money, credit is money, money begets money, honesty protects money, and the pursuit of all the virtues is tied to money. But what we see in Franklin's life and writings is *not* greed or egocentrism, because Franklin

---

[58] We must notice that what a person or group of people regards as economic rationality is dependent on values and assumptions about life that they bring into work and economic activity. Work is a necessity given to all people by creation; *how* we work is heavily influenced by our broader philosophy of life.

[59] In all of this discussion, worldly asceticism, sometimes called *intramundane* asceticism, is contrasted with types of religious asceticism that may involve some type of religiously motivated withdrawal from society or self-denying religious exercises that provide no societal benefit. These other types of religious self-denial are often called *extramundane* asceticism.

strongly rejected a self-indulgent lifestyle. Money is the result of diligence, excellence, and virtue in performing one's duties. Furthermore, an ascetic, self-denying way of life and work is needed to attain this excellence. But the goal is personal excellence and the attainment of moral virtue, not the money which usually results from the pursuit of excellence.

In contrast with Franklin's way of life, Weber suggests we consider a more traditional way from the past. Traditionally, if an employer paid employees according to how much they accomplished, it would be counterproductive to increase the pay for a unit of work because the worker would think in terms of needing a fixed amount of money to pay his regular bills. A larger amount of money for a unit of work would traditionally mean that the worker would simply work fewer hours per week so he could still pay his bills and enjoy more leisure. In contrast to the traditionalist, the modern capitalist worker would seize the opportunity to earn more money as part of the life of diligence and virtue, without using the increased earnings in a self-indulgent manner.

Weber saw an essential part of the religious background for the modern work ethic in Martin Luther's doctrine of calling (*Beruf* in German). Weber thought this was a genuinely new idea in western cultural history, that one's everyday worldly work and duties could carry deep religious significance. If people really believe that not only does everyday work have importance to God, but that all legitimate callings have equal worth before God and can glorify God, there will be significant economic consequences. But, according to Weber, Luther tended to interpret the radical idea of callings inside a traditionalist understanding of economics. Therefore, the social effects of Luther's doctrine of calling were limited. Only among the Calvinists and Puritans did the Protestant doctrine of calling reach its fullest effects.

Typical of Calvinism, according to Weber, is the doctrine of divine predestination, according to which God preordains which people are destined to eternal salvation and which people are destined to eternal damnation. This doctrine, thought Weber, gives rise to an unprecedented "inner loneliness" of the single individual, as each person has to face his eternal destiny on his own without the help of any other person, the Church, or the sacraments. Calvin may have had assurance of eternal salvation and may have taught that such assurance is possible to other believers, but ordinary people in the Calvinist tradition tended to become rational, unemotional, disillusioned individualists living in spiritual isolation from each other inside the same church, as they faced their uncertain eternal destiny. But there is a psychological necessity for people to have some means of recognizing a state of grace, whether in themselves or in others. This recognition of a state of grace was by means of evident and steadily increasing activity for the glory of God. Such activity was not really a means of earning salvation, but it was a means of recognizing if a person was in a state of grace. Therefore, people endeavored mightily to prove by means of a worldly asceticism that they were in a state of grace and eternally destined for heaven. Pietism and Methodism have some theological differences from Calvinism and are not quite so unemotional, but they have a similar inner logic of demonstrating that a person is in a state of grace by means of systematically planning his life according to the will of God. Therefore, Pietism and Methodism have a relation to worldly asceticism and capitalism similar to that found in Calvinism.

As a theologian who has learned much from John Calvin, I would insist that Weber seriously misunderstood the Calvinist doctrines of salvation and predestination. Calvin and the better theologians of the Reformed tradition have rejoiced in assurance of justification and have written eloquently about the joy of knowing God's fatherly care, themes that are the total denial of "inner loneliness." The Christian life has routinely been described as a life of gratitude for the gifts of creation and redemption. However, Weber's description of the Protestant work ethic and its historical influence is approximately right.

While commenting on Weber's interpretation of Calvin, John T. McNeill, the distinguished historian of Calvinism, concisely summarized the Protestant work ethic:

> There is no realm of life that is exempt from obligation of service to God and man. ... The layman's calling is not secular or religiously indifferent. We are not our own: every Christian is to live as one dedicated. ... Calvin makes much of humility and the abandonment of assumptions of superiority and all self-love as basic to Christian behavior. In grateful response to God's love, we love and serve our neighbor, who, good or bad, attractive or repulsive, bears the image of God. ... Calvin would have us abandon all thought of seeking material prosperity for ourselves. Whatever worldly goods we handle or possess, our function with them is one of stewardship. We and our possessions together belong to God. This view involves the hallowing of each man's vocation. It is "the post assigned," to be faithfully exercised.
>
> Calvin's insistence on diligence and frugality, his horror at waste of time or of goods, his permitting interest on money under strict limitations of equity and charity, and his similarly guarded permission of a change of vocation

are justly held to have contributed something to the development of capitalistic industry and business.[60]

A second appraisal of the influence of Protestantism on economic life comes from Gerhard Simon. Simon very carefully clarified that Calvin's ethics were not those of the brutal capitalism of the later era of industrialization. Instead, "Calvin's aspiration in this arena was entirely oriented toward helping the poor."[61] And Calvin thought that the poor were best helped within a context of a broadly flourishing economy.[62] As parts of his economic ethics, Calvin rejected the idea of an unchanging "just price" for goods (which could easily prevent market forces from bringing prices down to what poor people could pay for daily needs), allowed payment of interest on business loans under strict rules (thereby promoting the start of new business), and taught people to work hard and consistently without increasing consumption or luxury, leading to saving and investment in future business. This was such a marked change in the way Christians talked about business and work ethics that, claims Simon, "one can talk about a turning point in the flow of western thought and culture."[63] Therefore, "Calvin's command to simultaneously work, save, and invest gradually became the foundation of a new economic system."[64]

Though McNeill and Simon disagreed with Weber's interpretation of Calvin's theology, they agreed with Weber on two fundamental points: generally, how people go about work and business is heavily influenced by

---

[60] McNeil, p. 221.
[61] Gerhard Simon, "Bibel und Börse: Die Religiösen Wurzeln des Kapitalismus," *Archiv für Kulturgeschichte* 66 (1984) pp. 87-115. Here p. 112. All quotations from Gerhard Simon are borrowed from Thomas Schirrmacher, *Ethik*, Band 3: *Wirtschaft, Kirche, und Staat* (Hamburg: RVB and Nürnberg: VTR, 2001), pp. 151-154.
[62] To appreciate Calvin's concern, we must not forget that most of the population of Europe in his day lived in oppressively harsh poverty, and even if all the wealth of the upper classes had been widely distributed, there would have been very little relief from that poverty. In this light, Calvin read biblical texts such as 1 Thess. 4:11 ("Make it your ambition to lead a quiet life, to mind your own business, and to work with your hands.") and Eph. 4:28 ("He who has been stealing must steal no longer, but must work, doing something useful with his own hands, that he may have something to share with those in need."), and Calvin concluded that the only possible way out of poverty was for his people to work more consistently and more wisely. The only solution to the poverty he saw was the generation of more wealth.
[63] *Ibid,* p. 113. German to English translations by Prof. Johnson.
[64] *Ibid,* p. 104.

moral and cultural values in which religious beliefs play a decisive role. Specifically, the Protestant work ethic has made a decisive contribution to economic development in multiple parts of the world.

In our historical setting in post-communist Europe, we must notice the complete disagreement of Max Weber with Karl Marx. Marx claimed that religion, ethics, and cultural values are entirely the result of economic factors, whereas Weber thought that religion, ethics, and cultural values are independent causes of individual economic decisions and the economies of nations. Marx and Weber offer us totally opposite views of the relation between economic life and cultural values; they present a complete contrast in terms of the relation between business and the philosophy of life held by individuals or an entire society.

Today we all know we cannot understand twentieth- century history without knowing something about Marxism; Marxist ideas changed the course of history in a tragic way. If Marxist ideas can have a massive influence on history, then other philosophies of life, religions, and systems of values can also change the course of history. This means Marx was wrong on the very important question of the relation of moral/cultural values to economic and political life.[65] Ironically, Marxist history confirms my claims about the role of ideas, beliefs, and moral values in society in a manner that strongly contradicts central claims of Marx. A Marxist should see Reformation theology and ethics as merely the superstructure of life resulting from distinctive economic relations. History shows that religious and cultural value systems cause economic transitions.[66]

This insight into society is crucial for our assessment of the world economic crisis. If we fail to reconsider how different philosophies of life contribute either to healthy economic growth or to an economic crisis, we will thoughtlessly follow Karl Marx on a most disputable point in his philosophy, even if our politics are democratic and our economics are market-oriented. If we ignore the values and convictions that contributed to our economic crisis, we would be like the person who thinks a lot of aspirin is

---

[65]   I am very grateful to have learned from Michael Novak to see Marx and Weber as presenting directly opposing views on the relationship between culture and economics while I was preparing and writing the special Russian language introduction and footnotes for his *Spirit of Democratic Capitalism* (Minsk, Belarus: Luchi Sophii, 1997). My participation in this publication of a book by a leading Roman Catholic social economic theorist is an example of the positive interaction between Catholics and Protestants in the realm of social-economic theory.

[66]   A friend who is an investment manager has commented that Calvin and Marx represent the real alternatives of how to view the way economies work.

the right solution to a terrible alcoholic hangover every morning. We must look at the problem more courageously.

Abraham Kuyper, the Dutch Reformed theologian of a century ago, did much to develop the theory of Sphere Sovereignty as a framework for understanding society. Our Roman Catholic friends have further developed this idea, and I would like to borrow it back from them.[67]

In a modern society there are always at least three spheres or societal systems that continually interact with each other: the business/economic, the legal/political, and the moral/cultural systems. Each of the three major systems in society is heavily dependent on the other two systems functioning in a healthy manner. This is interdependence. A healthy economy is dependent on health in both the moral/cultural system and in the legal/political system. A healthy legal/political system depends on healthy cultural and economic systems. And a healthy moral/cultural system depends on healthy economic and political systems. While the preaching of the Christian gospel of reconciliation with God is the leading task of the church, as the carrier of the Christian message, the church also plays and should play a massive role in the formation of the moral/cultural system. Culture always goes beyond moral rules and values to include the definition of human nature and destiny, a subject about which the church has much to say, always in competition with other definitions, whether Marxist, libertarian, or consumerist. While the political and economic spheres are properly separate from the cultural sphere, human activity in the political and economic spheres is *always* guided by our understanding of what it means to be a human being and by a related set of moral values and practical principles. In this sense, political life and economic life are both dependent on the cultural sphere of life for direction and guidance.

The moral/cultural sphere of life will never be truly empty; there will always be some moral/cultural content, some definition of human nature and destiny. The problem is that the content of the moral/cultural sphere may be poorly chosen, perhaps with self-destructive values or with definitions of human nature and destiny that do not fit who we really are. Such a failure of the moral/cultural sphere of society will lead to terrible results in the political and economic systems. The failure of Marxist Communism was a result of a description of human nature and destiny in communist ideology that did not honestly fit with human nature and experience. We must never forget that moral/cultural values and the understanding of human destiny are simultaneously philosophical *and* religious matters. Our

---

[67] See Richard John Neuhaus, *Doing Well and Doing Good: The Challenge to the Christian Capitalist* (Doubleday, 1992).

understanding of penultimate cultural matters (human nature and destiny) always stands in dialogue with our understanding of the ultimate, the nature of ultimate being, which is properly the realm of religion. This is the pivotal connection among religions, culture, and economics.

When we talk about the moral/cultural sphere of life, we must never forget the multi-faceted relationship between faith and culture. The Christian faith stands in an answering relationship to culture, speaking to the deepest anxieties of each culture. The Christian faith should also have a critical relationship to each culture, attempting to stand as representatives of the Ultimate Social Critic. Additionally, the Christian faith must attempt to contribute something to each culture in which the church exists, articulating a rich perspective on human nature and destiny as an effective voice in the moral/cultural system.[68] When we Christians contribute to the moral/cultural system in a society, on the one hand, we will properly describe much of what we want to say as simply biblical teaching or Christian ethics, which we see as given by God. This ethical teaching is inseparable from our faith. On the other hand, once these ideas are explained, they often achieve an authoritative status for many people, even if those people do not share our Christians beliefs. Christian moral/cultural convictions can have a wide influence among people who do not claim to be Christians and may not know the source of their moral convictions. This was a key element in Weber's observations about the historical influence of the Protestant work ethic. In theological terms, because of God's common grace and revelation through nature, people often accept humane moral principles that tend to preserve and protect human well-being, whether or not the people acknowledge that these moral principles come from God. Therefore, many Christian moral convictions can both have direct intuitive validity and also be capable of rational/scientific documentation, even among people who do not (yet) accept Christian beliefs about God and salvation. This moral content may seem to some to be somewhat separable from personal faith; this is not because God is irrelevant. It is because God is active in a twofold manner: on the one hand, through redemption by faith in the life of believers, and on the other hand, as the Sustainer and Ruler over all.[69]

Today we need a renewal of the moral/cultural sphere of society in relation to business, economics, and work ethics. Therefore, I would propose

---

[68] For more on faith and culture, see my "Christ and Culture," MBS Text 79, available at www.bucer.eu.

[69] For more on this topic, see my essay "The Twofold Work of God in the World," MBS Text 102, available at www.bucer.eu.

the following 20 theses as part of the content we need in the moral/cultural sphere to have healthy economies. Each thesis is organically tied to the Christian faith or arises from the faith, and there are biblical sources for many of these ideas. But most of these ideas are not directly about God or salvation, so even atheists or adherents of other religions may be able to accept many of them. These 20 theses describe human nature and destiny, with supporting moral principles that fit with this view of human nature. Each is worthy of a long explanation, which is not possible here.

1. Human beings are filled with creative potential; each person can and should take the initiative to do something significant with the potential he has been given. Wise business and economic structures will seek to unlock this potential.
2. Greed, laziness, and dishonesty have roots in our fallen condition which are far deeper than any economic system or situation. Businesses and society should be structured to restrain our vices, use these vices for the common good, or reduce the destructive power of these vices.
3. Loving our neighbors as ourselves is the proper framework for work and business. We should seek to provide for our own needs by means of genuinely serving the needs of our neighbors.
4. The alienation from ourselves, from each other, and from our work, so eloquently described by our Marxist friends, will not be overcome by a mere economic transition. Wise business structures may reduce this alienation in regard to the work place.
5. Our lives are not determined by an impersonal fate. God's sovereignty does not mean we should resign responsibility for the future. Whether we are Christians, atheists, or adherents of another religion, we must take responsibility for the future of our societies, including our economy.
6. History is not an eternal set of circles. History moves forward, so we should use our initiative and creativeness to develop the potential built into the world, under the providence of God.
7. The physical world is real and good, a place in which we can find significance, partly through our work. Believers will see this significance as part of the worship of God.
8. The promise that wealth will make us happy is false. Happiness will be found in significant relationships and activities, including work, hobbies, family, community organizations, and worship.
9. Giving to help someone in need, rather than buying something for ourselves, will contribute to our life satisfaction.

10. Entertainment and consumption will not fill our inner need for ultimate meaning.
11. Material goods do not belong to me as an individual; they belong to me as a member of a family, including children and grandchildren. Responsible economic decisions will reflect this multi-generational view of life.
12. Honesty really is the best policy. Not only is honesty expected by God, it is a key to human well-being in all relationships and sectors of society.
13. Providing jobs to people can be as great an act of love as is humanitarian aid, since it provides people the opportunity to actualize their potential.
14. It is possible to carry on business without exploiting other people. Honest buying and selling generally helps both parties; honest financial transactions are not exploitative.
15. While it is often possible to recognize prices that are exploitative, it is not possible to identify enduring "fair prices" in the manner of some medieval Christians.
16. While not all loans are immoral, some loans are immoral, and many loans have been unwise for borrowers and lenders. Borrowing is a morally serious undertaking which requires serious deliberation.
17. Laziness is a serious vice which destroys business, economies, families, and communities.
18. Intact families are an important end in themselves, but they also play a very significant role in total economic and societal well-being. Family breakdown causes economic problems in multiple ways.
19. Both management and labor must accept the discipline of the marketplace, which requires continually improving quality and service for lower prices.
20. People generally know a lot about right and wrong, more than they like to admit to knowing. Business life stands under the same moral demands as all sectors of our lives.

Because of the organic unity of thought and action in human life, ideas have consequences. Good ideas have good consequences, and bad ideas have bad consequences, including bad economic consequences. These 20 theses can help provide a framework for following the historic Protestant values of diligence, honesty, family loyalty, creativity, and thrift. Following such values can lead to a renewal of the moral/cultural sphere of society, which can support a healthy economy. Christians should practice these values as part of their worship of God. I hope all our neighbors will practice these values as good practical wisdom and also consider our distinctly Christian claim that it is really God who wants us to live in this manner.

Chapter VI: The Moral Crisis of the West

Though I wrote this essay more than 20 years ago, when I was living in a different place and carrying different responsibilities, I am more convinced than ever that our understanding of human nature is central to most of the big questions facing western culture.[70] Our civilization lacks a coherent explanation of what we are as humans, and this unanswered question casts a shadow across politics, business, finance, education, the arts, and medicine. The French political philosopher Chantel Delsol writes, "The twentieth century is the story of the dismantling of the idea of humanity, a process that gave rise to the disintegration of the essential common world that took so many centuries to build. This disintegration served as the prerequisite and foundation for the possibility of totalitarianism."[71] Further, "if humanity is no longer sacred, everything becomes possible, from hatred to mass assassination."[72] Delsol sees the problem of adequately describing our humanness as cultural, political, moral, and ultimately religious, for, "perhaps the biblical tale does indeed represent the only guarantee against the temptation to displace the human species. It is nothing more than a story, one might object. Yet dignity does not exist without this story, for dignity was discovered or invented along with it, and all our efforts to establish other foundations have turned out to be very poor substitutes."[73]

One of the urgent intellectual needs of our generation is a restatement of a biblically informed view of what humans are, done in a manner that shows how the biblical view of a person relates to our various cultural problems. Without such a new proclamation of our humanness, our societies will continue to see humans as only biological/economic creatures (a tendency seen too often both in the political left and the political right), which will make the practical solutions for our various economic and social problems even more difficult. Perhaps this little essay will prompt a reader to attempt such a restatement of the biblical view. In fact, this essay prompted me to make some further small attempts to describe humans in light of the biblical narrative. This includes "Adam and Eve: Who Are You?" which I wrote for the Theological Commission of Hope for Europe

---

[70] When I wrote this article I was pastor of Hope Evangelical Church (PCA) in Iowa City, Iowa (USA), where I also taught ethics at Kirkwood College.

[71] Chantal Delsol, *The Unlearned Lesson of the Twentieth Century: An Essay on Late Modernity* (Wilmington: ISI Books, 2006), p. 15.

[72] Delsol, p. 21.

[73] Delsol, p. 21.

(2002), "Who or What Is Man?" which I wrote for the World Reformed Fellowship (2003), and *Human Rights: A Christian Primer* (Bonn: Culture and Science Pub., 2008), which I wrote for the World Evangelical Alliance and the International Institute for Religious Freedom.

The following text was originally published in *Presbyterion*, 17:2, 1991, a theological journal of Covenant Theological Seminary in St. Louis. Martin Bucer Seminary then gratefully reused this text for study materials. Since writing this essay I have been convinced by a more careful study of Romans 1 that one of the themes of God's general revelation, by means of which he both sustains human life and calls people to repentance, is the reality of human dignity, but like all the truths people learn from God's general revelation, this truth can be largely suppressed from consciousness. But because this truth is contained in God's general revelation (as well as in special revelation in Christ and the Bible), it was and is possible for this truth to be communicated from the Christian community into our surrounding cultures.

The Moral Crisis of the West

Reflections from Helmut Thielicke and Francis Schaeffer

About nine blocks from our home in Iowa City, Iowa stands the Emma Goldman Clinic for Women. The work of this clinic contributes to the grisly statistic that there are 2.5 or 3 abortions per live birth in the Iowa City area.[74] Even if John Naisbitt and Patricia Aburdene are right, that the immediate future looks very bright in economic, political, and artistic terms,[75] we face a moral crisis of vast proportions. The situation approximates that of the prophet Amos a few decades before the destruction of Israel – a political/economic boom during a moral/spiritual collapse – and cries out for an adequate response from the church.

A precise analysis of this moral crisis is crucial, for how we analyze the crisis will undoubtedly influence how we respond to it. Two recent Protestant theologians who have reflected on the moral crisis of the West are Francis Schaeffer and Helmut Thielicke. While there are differences in their assessments of modern culture, Schaeffer emphasizing the loss of rationality and moral absolutes and Thielicke focusing on the problem of autonomous spheres of life, there is substantial agreement on one major

---

[74] *American Family Association Journal* (July, 1988), p 11. In 1980, the last date for which I had precise statistics, the ratio was 2.84 to 1.

[75] *Megatrends Two Thousand* (New York: Morrow, 1990).

point: Western culture is endangered by its reduced view of human dignity, which is, in turn, a symptom of the modern secular worldview. Thielicke's and Schaeffer's explanations of the origins of this problem complement each other and together suggest a comprehensive response. We will begin our comparison with Thielicke.

Helmut Thielicke

Thielicke contrasts two views of human dignity: the Christian view, which emphasizes "alien dignity," versus what he calls non-Christian functionalism.[76] The term "alien dignity" is borrowed from Martin Luther.[77] It means that people have a dignity that does not come from anything within themselves, a personal dignity that arises from how God views that person. A deaf, mute, blind, retarded quadriplegic has infinite value in God's eyes, because Christ died for him/her.[78] That person is the apple of God's eye, and anyone who touches that person must do so in kindness or risk incurring God's anger.

We should notice that Thielicke's term "alien dignity" is analogous to the alien righteousness we receive when we are justified by faith. We are justified not because we have any achieved or inherent righteousness, but because Christ's alien righteousness is credited to us by God. Likewise, the person with no achieved or inherent dignity has dignity credited to him/her by God.

Typical non-Christian functionalism makes a person's value dependent on his function in society. If a person makes a large contribution to society, he is valued highly. If he makes only a small contribution to society, he is valued only a little. If he makes no contribution or is a burden to society, he is to be disposed of, provided the public outcry is not too great.[79]

Thielicke claims that it is typical of modern secularism to have a functional approach to human value and dignity. Each worldview takes some dimension of creation and interprets all of reality in light of it, making each

---

[76] *The Evangelical Faith*, vol. 1: *Prolegomena: The Relation of Theology to Modern Thought Forms*, trans. G. W. Bromiley (Grand Rapids: Wm. B. Eerdmans Publishing Co., 1974), p. 382. *The Evangelical Faith*, vol. 2: *The Doctrine of God and of Christ*, trans. G. W. Bromiley (Grand Rapids: Wm. B. Eerdnans Publishing Co., 1977), p. 46.

[77] *Theological Ethics*, vol. 1: Foundations, trans. and ed. William H. Lazareth (Grand Rapids: Wm. B. Eerdmans Pub. Co., 1979), pp. 171–194.

[78] *Ibid.*, p 21.

[79] *Nihilism: Its Origin and Nature – with a Christian Answer*, trans. John W. Doberstein (New York: Harper and Brother, 1961), p. 84.

a different type of idolatry.[80] Marxism made the economic substructure of society its idol,[81] while National Socialism picked the German race and blood. People are then valued in light of the aspect of creation that has been idolized. Marxists value people who are economically productive, while Nazis value people with pure Aryan blood. As much as Marxists and Nazis are different, they join in denying alien dignity and valuing people only in terms of their function in society.

The functional view of human dignity has had hideous effects in the twentieth century. The Holocaust was closest to Thielicke's experience.[82] Millions of people who could not make a social contribution valued by the Nazis were eliminated. Sexual abuse and promiscuity are also related to a functional view of human dignity, for these reduce the other person to a function, not seeing the other as a whole person before God.[83] Similarly, the practice of abortion follows quite naturally from a denial of alien dignity.[84]

The way in which one comes to "see" the alien dignity of another is by faith in Christ. When we come to faith, the Holy Spirit miraculously opens our eyes to see God's grace. He also opens our eyes to see Christ in our brother, to see that Christ died for the other person.[85] Awareness of the alien dignity in others enables Christians to love their neighbors and even their enemies.[86] The new eyes given by the Spirit lead believers to care for and protect the non-functional members of society rather than discard them.

Awareness of the alien dignity of each individual was once a driving force in western culture, leading it to its heights. And even after secularism displaced Christianity as the dominant worldview, the power of the notion of alien dignity continued for a time. But today the cultural effects of an awareness of alien dignity are rapidly disappearing.[87]

---

[80] *Nihilism*, pp. 17–20.
[81] Thielicke's fascinating critique of Marxism appears largely in *The Freedom of the Christian Man: A Christian Confrontation with the Secular Gods*, trans. John W. Doberstein (New York: Harper & Row, 1963), and in *The Hidden Question of God*, trans. G. W. Bromiley (Grand Rapids: Wm. B. Eerdmans Co., 1977).
[82] "Why the Holocaust?," *Christianity Today* 22/8 (January 27, 1978): 8–14.
[83] Thielicke, *Theological Ethics*, vol. 3: *Sex*, trans. J. W. Doberstein (Grand Rapids: Wm. B. Eerdmans, 1979), pp. 20–26.
[84] *Ibid.*, pp. 230–232.
[85] *The Evangelical Faith*, vol. 3: *Theology of the Spirit*, trans. G. W. Bromiley (Grand Rapids: Wm. B. Eerdmans, 1982), pp. 54–65.
[86] Thielicke, *Theological Ethics*, 3: 32.
[87] Thielicke, *The Evangelical Faith*, 2: 46–47.

Francis Schaeffer

Schaeffer also frequently contrasts Christian and non-Christian views of human dignity. Over and over he argues that the Christian has a basis for seeing himself and others as having dignity and personality by virtue of having been created in the image of God. Non-Christian systems, on the other hand, have no place for human dignity or personality. This is so, even though non-Christians experience themselves and others as personal. It contrasts to Thielicke's theological interpretations of the problem. Schaeffer offers an historical sketch of how the problem arose, coupled with an analysis of the results of anti-Christian views of human nature.

Modern man, from Leonardo Da Vinci to the present, begins from himself (not from God's revelation), with Man as the only integration point, and tries to find all knowledge, meaning, and value on the basis of human inquiry alone.[88] Like Michelangelo's statues, modern man wants to tear himself from the rock and be autonomous and free. But with Hegel and Kierkegaard came a division between rationality (which had proven incapable of producing an integrated and meaningful view of life) and all that is distinctly human, e.g., purpose, love, morals, personality, dignity.[89] The distinctly human was relegated to an irrational leap in the dark. Moreover, many modern naturalists take a further step, reducing everything to mechanics and particulars alone.[90] But without universals, no meaning or morals or anything distinctly human remains. All that is left, in the modern secular mind, is a cause-effect nexus encompassing everything, including man. Schaeffer often calls this "the uniformity of cause and effect in a closed system." This is especially seen in the social sciences. Ironically, the line of thought that began with man's quest for freedom ends with the complete loss of human dignity, as seen in Skinner's behaviorism.[91] In Schaeffer's terms, modern man has fallen below the line of despair because he "has tried to build a system out from himself, but this system has come to the place where there is not room in the universe for man."[92]

---

[88] *The Complete Works of Francis A. Schaeffer: A Christian Worldview*, vol. 1: *A Christian View of Philosophy and Culture* (Westchester, Illinois: Crossway Books, 1982), p. 9.

[89] *Ibid.*, p. 43.

[90] *The Complete Works of Francis A. Schaeffer: A Christian Worldview*, vol. 5: *A Christian View of the West* (Westchester, Illinois, Crossway Books, 1982), pp. 114, 115.

[91] Schaeffer, *Complete Works*, 1: 373–384.

[92] *Ibid.*, p. 32.

The cosmology that frequently accompanies modern humanism claims that impersonal matter and energy have always existed and that, with enough time and chance, man has evolved. But this view reduces man to an accidental bundle of molecules that is no different from any other bundle of molecules.[93] Humanity and personality disappear from view, for it is difficult to maintain belief in a real humanity while affirming an impersonal ultimate.

Unable to live with these results of western humanism, many moderns are turning to various forms of eastern mysticism and pantheism. But pantheism, rather than elevating man, also reduces him to the impersonal for "If we begin with less than personality, we must finally reduce personality to the impersonal."[94] Pantheism, like western naturalism, provides no ultimate basis for personality because it has no personal God in view. And pantheism has no basis for distinguishing man from nature. Again, there is no basis for human dignity.[95]

Such views, when held by large numbers of people, are not without result, for one's thought world inevitably shapes one's actions.[96] The chief result observable in today's society is a practical disregard for human life. While the bane of abortion represents a prime example of such disregard, other examples are not difficult to find, e.g., personal cruelty, racism, the abuse of genetic knowledge, infanticide, euthanasia, child abuse, incest, child pornography, slavery, and the notion that some lives are not worthy to be lived.[97]

Schaeffer recognizes that, despite what the secular prophets are saying, most people assume for themselves and others some measure of human dignity. He insists, however, that the only firm basis for such an assumption is what God has revealed in Scripture.

Conclusion

We may now draw some conclusions from this brief survey of Thielicke's and Schaefer's views on the question of human dignity. I would not want to defend every detail of the arguments of Thielicke or of Schaeffer. Thielicke, for example, may be mistaken to root the notion of alien dignity entirely in redemption rather than in creation, for this view betrays an undue

---

93   Schaeffer, *Complete Works*, 5: 180, 181; Schaeffer, *Complete Works*, 1: 358–362.
94   *Ibid.*, p. 286.
95   Schaeffer, *Complete Works*, 5: 18–19.
96   *Ibid.*, p. 83.
97   *Ibid.*, pp. 22–236, 281–293, 325–342.

dependence on Karl Barth's ethics, contains an implicit universalism, and seems much harder to argue in a pluralistic society than simply saying we are created in God's image. As for Schaeffer's approach, I, like many of his readers, sometimes wonder if he does not categorize some thinkers and the flow of western thought a little too neatly. In general, however, I think that Thielicke's theological interpretation and Schaeffer's historical sketch and analysis of the consequences of ideas can be readily joined as complementary. Thielicke has provided a key insight into the dynamics of modern secularist systems in his claim that they tend to view individuals in terms of the significance of their functions, as determined by whatever idolatry underlies the given system. From Schaeffer we gain the helpful observation that, while western rationalism provides no basis for human dignity or the experience of humanness, the escape from reason into irrationality also fails to give a basis for human dignity.

If the analyses of Schaeffer and Thielicke are, in the main, correct, it follows that our culture-wide moral crisis cannot be solved by direct political action alone. Thielicke's framework would emphasize evangelism and public preaching, for it is through conversion that one is enabled to see Christ in the other. And the preached Word tends to relativize idolatrous worldviews and their effects. Schaeffer's emphasis on the effects of ideas would emphasize training Christians in a comprehensive biblical worldview and in practicing the truth more consistently. At the same time, it would encourage Christians to challenge secularist worldviews by unveiling their presuppositions, their irrationality, and their incompatibility with normal experience. When such activities are conjoined with direct political involvement, which both Schaeffer and Thielicke practiced, the result will be a more comprehensive response to our time through evangelism, public preaching, careful teaching of Christians, Christian scholarship, lives marked by respect for human dignity, and political action to protect the defenseless and restrict the effects of the secular mind. And respond we must! For who knows if we, like Amos, are not seeing preliminary judgments that point to the wrath to come in our time?

Chapter VII: Interpreting the Ten Commandments

A Study in Special Hermeneutics

Deuteronomy 5 (New International Version [NIV])

The Ten Commandments

Moses summoned all Israel and said:

Hear, Israel, the decrees and laws I declare in your hearing today. Learn them and be sure to follow them. [2] The LORD our God made a covenant with us at Horeb. [3] It was not with our ancestors that the LORD made this covenant, but with us, with all of us who are alive here today. [4] The LORD spoke to you face to face out of the fire on the mountain. [5] (At that time I stood between the LORD and you to declare to you the word of the LORD, because you were afraid of the fire and did not go up the mountain.) And he said:

[6] "I am the LORD your God, who brought you out of Egypt, out of the land of slavery.

[7] "You shall have no other gods before me.

[8] "You shall not make for yourself an image in the form of anything in heaven above or on the earth beneath or in the waters below. [9] You shall not bow down to them or worship them; for I, theLORD your God, am a jealous God, punishing the children for the sin of the parents to the third and fourth generation of those who hate me, [10] but showing love to a thousand generations of those who love me and keep my commandments.

[11] "You shall not misuse the name of the LORD your God, for the LORD will not hold anyone guiltless who misuses his name.

[12] "Observe the Sabbath day by keeping it holy, as the LORD your God has commanded you. [13] Six days you shall labor and do all your work, [14] but the seventh day is a sabbath to the LORD your God. On it you shall not do any work, neither you, nor your son or daughter, nor your male or female servant, nor your ox, your donkey or any of your animals, nor any foreigner residing in your towns, so that your male and female servants may rest, as you do. [15] Remember that you were

slaves in Egypt and that the LORD your God brought you out of there with a mighty hand and an outstretched arm. Therefore the LORD your God has commanded you to observe the Sabbath day.

16 "Honor your father and your mother, as the LORD your God has commanded you, so that you may live long and that it may go well with you in the land the LORD your God is giving you.

17 "You shall not murder.

18 "You shall not commit adultery.

19 "You shall not steal.

20 "You shall not give false testimony against your neighbor.

21 "You shall not covet your neighbor's wife. You shall not set your desire on your neighbor's house or land, his male or female servant, his ox or donkey, or anything that belongs to your neighbor."

22 These are the commandments the LORD proclaimed in a loud voice to your whole assembly there on the mountain from out of the fire, the cloud and the deep darkness; and he added nothing more. Then he wrote them on two stone tablets and gave them to me.

23 When you heard the voice out of the darkness, while the mountain was ablaze with fire, all the leaders of your tribes and your elders came to me. 24 And you said, "The LORD our God has shown us his glory and his majesty, and we have heard his voice from the fire. Today we have seen that a person can live even if God speaks with them. 25 But now, why should we die? This great fire will consume us, and we will die if we hear the voice of the LORD our God any longer. 26 For what mortal has ever heard the voice of the living God speaking out of fire, as we have, and survived? 27 Go near and listen to all that the LORD our God says. Then tell us whatever the LORD our God tells you. We will listen and obey."

28 The LORD heard you when you spoke to me, and the LORD said to me, "I have heard what this people said to you. Everything they said was good. 29 Oh, that their hearts would be inclined to fear me and keep all my commands always, so that it might go well with them and their children forever!

30 "Go, tell them to return to their tents. 31 But you stay here with me so that I may give you all the commands, decrees and laws you are to teach them to follow in the land I am giving them to possess."

32 So be careful to do what the LORD your God has commanded you; do not turn aside to the right or to the left. 33 Walk in obedience to all that the LORD your God has commanded you, so that you may live and prosper and prolong your days in the land that you will possess."

People often have strong feelings about the Ten Commandments. Just a few years ago Americans observed the strange spectacle of a national judge ordering a state judge to remove an artistic portrayal of the Decalogue from a courthouse. But then a large group of citizens gathered to protest the removal. Both those in power and those on the streets had strong and opposed feelings about God's law, which may serve as a good illustration about how our world feels about the rules written in stone: some love them, some hate them, and many love and hate them at the same time. Probably all of us know that God's Commandments are crucial to the Christian response to the overwhelming moral relativism which is wreaking havoc in so much of global society while we also sense that God's law strikes deep existential issues related to guilt and acceptance within the human heart.

The intense and contradictory feelings about the Decalogue, and especially the hatred of the Commandments, can easily arise from serious misinterpretations. Surely there are serious misunderstandings of each of the commandments, but there are also serious misinterpretations of the Decalogue as a whole. During almost 20 years of teaching philosophy and religion in secular universities, I have repeatedly heard two misunderstandings of God's law as a whole. The first says that these commandments are arbitrary and irrational, having no connection with human nature or human well-being so that they do not contribute to human happiness. Though it is seldom stated so directly, many seem to think that if one wants to be self-destructive and have a miserable and messed up life, one should simply follow these old-fashioned, irrational rules. This first misunderstanding makes it important to emphasize the organic connection between the Decalogue and the natural moral law or created moral order which preserves human well-being. The second misinterpretation assumes that the main purpose of the Ten Commandments is to teach people how to earn God's favor. If you want to go to heaven, if you want to be sure you are accepted by God, if you want to overcome your guilt and sin, it is said, you must keep the Commandments. This is the most common misinterpretation of the Decalogue as a whole, and it is so common because it is so deeply rooted in our sinful nature, the nature that keeps on whispering, "If we need to be saved, we can do it ourselves." Because of this second, standard misunderstanding of the purpose of the law, we must always emphasize the contrast between law and gospel. The gospel tells us that we are justified and fully accepted before God by faith alone, a faith that trusts in the promise of God for forgiveness based on the death and resurrection of Christ. Thereby the gospel also tells us that the proper purposes of the law must be something other than teaching us how to earn God's favor.

So what are the proper purposes of God's law, if not to earn salvation? There are at least three proper purposes or uses of the moral law that stand up to critical scrutiny, and none of them has to do with earning salvation. 1. God's law shows us our sin and need for the gospel. This is commonly called the "theological use" or "converting use" of God's law. Whether at the beginning of our life of faith or on a continuing basis over many years of living by faith, God's law drives us to cry out, "God, be merciful to me, a sinner." By showing us our sin, the law drives us to love the gospel ever more strongly, for in the gospel we learn about forgiveness, justification, and adoption as God's children. 2. The law also restrains our sin so we do not act out all of the sinful tendencies in our hearts. This is sometimes called the "political" use of the law, using the ancient meaning of the word "polis," which is community. Our sin is so powerful that if it is not re-strained, the communities for which God created us are easily turned into the total chaos of the "war of all against all." But God's law comes to us in a wide variety of ways, some not so pure, including conscience, reason, civil law, family, and Scripture, with the effect of normally restraining our sin at least partially. In this way, it is a primary means of God's common or civilizing grace, which makes life in society possible most of the time. For this reason, this is also called the "civil" use of the moral law. 3. The law of God also provides a norm or standard for the life of gratitude. Because of the tremendous grace we have been given in the gospel, our entire lives should be an expression of thankfulness to God, but this gratitude needs a specific structure and direction. This we find in the commands in the Scrip-tures, which are not only the condemning law but also, by the Spirit, the empowering directives and descriptions of the new possibilities for believ-ers. The law describes the restored life of gratitude which God wants us to live for his glory.

We must notice and say over and over again that none of the proper us-es of God's law have anything to do with earning God's favor or salvation. There are multiple valid and good uses of God's law, and in life experience the various uses may tend to slide together, but earning our way to heaven is not a proper use of God's law.

If very strong feelings about God's law are often connected with mis-taken interpretations, as well as with mistaken uses, of God's law, we should try to articulate clear principles of interpretation and application. The following seven principles have been developed by a range of theolo-gians, ethicists, and Bible scholars. They are presented here as a kind of compendium or short study for those who may not be able to read extensively in Christian ethics or hermeneutics. Serious students will want to read much further from the literature listed at the end.

I. The negative implies the positive.

Many of the commandments are phrased in the negative, "You shall not ..." From that starting point a mature and morally sensitive reader can normally see the positive expectations of a particular commandment, those actions we *should* take. Since God did not make us to be robots or computers, apparently he wants us to actively engage in the process of considering the positive demand implied by the negative prohibition. For example, Commandment 6 says, "You shall not murder." If you are able to read this article, you probably also have the ability to deduce the positive demand of Commandment 6, that God wants us to protect and care for the lives of people. Even if no murder detective is hot on your trail, you are not finished with this commandment. We are required to treat the people we meet as images or reflections of the Lord himself. But even that does not complete our obligations. We have to think about society very generally. What is there that we can do to protect and care for the lives of other people in our city, our country, and beyond? Obedience to this commandment goes far beyond avoiding murder. It should make us consider long and hard what we need to do to protect people's lives and safety.

There is a direct spiritual line from reflecting on this commandment to actions such as working to abolish slavery, starting orphanages, providing disaster assistance, and ending abortion. If the negative prohibition implies and assumes the positive demand, we can spend a lifetime learning to obey the will of God. If we are morally sensitive readers of the Decalogue, we must do something like this with most of the ten. We will begin a process of thinking, consideration, and action that can change our lives, families, and communities.

II. The direct prohibition of an action makes improper moral rationalizing more difficult.

This is a moral consideration that also has to do with the negative phrasing of the commandments. One can understand this by contrasting a very general moral principle such as "private property" with God's commandment, "You shall not steal." Of course, the general moral principle is very good and has significant value in life and society. But in a moment of weakness or temptation, it is much more powerful for us sinners to have the explicit negative command echoing in the back of our minds. The commandment confronts us precisely at the point of our weakness. It puts a name on the sinful act we might otherwise prefer to leave unnamed and unnoticed, and we sinners would prefer to leave our sins unnamed and unnoticed. Of course, the negative confrontation is uncomfortable for us, but precisely this moral discomfort may be what is necessary to restrain some of our destructive instincts. Many of the commandments can be rephrased as positive, general moral principles, and as suggested above, this is a good thing to do. If done properly, this will be extremely challenging, even life-changing. But this must never replace the negative, confrontational format in which God chose to give the commands. All too often our sinful nature would seek to find good sounding rational/ethical reasons for doing what is simply wrong. Then we need to be confronted by the divine "You shall not!"

III. If we interpret the commandments properly, we will be confronted in our sinfulness.

If God had given the commandments to Adam and Eve prior to the fall into sin, the disturbing word "NOT" might have been avoided. But since the fall, all of us, the sons and daughters of Adam and Eve, need to be continually confronted with our sin. One could say we need to get to know ourselves as God sees us, and that means getting to know ourselves as sinners. This self-knowledge is not something that one learns simply and quickly, like a bit of information; it is a continual process of learning that lasts a lifetime, something like the process of learning wisdom.

The commandment says "You shall not," to which a dark voice in our souls sometimes still replies, "But I want to." In this experience we encounter one of the darkest sides of sin: sometimes we want to do something simply because it is wrong. This leads to the unpleasant collision with the little word "*not.*"

This experience is a key that helps us understand the continually recurring controversy about the public display of the Ten Commandments. If one reads the American legal documents surrounding this controversy, one will probably find competing theories about the separation of church and state. Some think that as long as the state does not directly promote or prohibit a particular church, and as long as no church is controlling the state, we have enough separation of church and state. Others seem to want almost no contact between any state agency and anything vaguely religious, even symbols or terminology, perhaps an impossible goal. But this disagreement might be a quiet debate among scholars were it not for the intense reactions people have to the Ten Commandments. The law of God makes us feel guilty because we are guilty; there is no escaping this unpleasant truth. If we are believers, it pushes us to more deeply appreciate the gospel of forgiveness in Christ. But the person who does not accept forgiveness in Christ may simply become angry, and this anger may be taken out on people who have a different reaction to God's law.

IV. The Ten Commandments sharpen and clarify God's law given through creation.

We should normally speak of two revelations from God, his special revelation through Christ and Scripture and his general revelation through creation. There are very significant differences in content between the two revelations: special revelation has Christ and the gospel at its very center, whereas general revelation contains only vague hints about grace; general revelation gives us a sense of God's majesty and holiness, whereas special revelation gives us much more specific information about God's character and also explains his mercy; by special revelation God's law was specifically written on stone at Sinai, whereas by general revelation his law was partly written in the human heart and mind. This means that even if people do not acknowledge it and do not like it, they know something about the demands of God's law. This knowledge comes through conscience, through feelings for the needs of others, through thinking about what is rational for people to do, through relationships, and through the everyday demands of life. We could call it an unrecognized demand, because some do not want to recognize that the demand comes from the Almighty. It is this unrecognized demand that is a primary means of God's common, civilizing grace that helps keep life in society somewhat humane and which also can prepare people to see their need for the gospel.

Because of this general revelation of God's law, also called the natural moral law, the Ten Commandments are not exactly new or news. Reading or hearing the Decalogue is more like taking passive knowledge and making it active or like taking subconscious knowledge and making it conscious. For some it may be like remembering a pleasant dream; for others it is more like being pushed back into a frightening nightmare because of the demanding Law Giver they have hoped to avoid.

People just know that murder, stealing, lying, and adultery are wrong, even when they try to defend their foolish actions. People just know we should practice love, justice, honesty, faithfulness, and courage, even if some may not want to admit that we know. This is because of God's general revelation. We should not talk as if the Ten Commandments primarily give us new information that we did not have before. The written law of God takes the demand that may have previously been unrecognized and makes it more clear, conscious, and precise, while also emphasizing that this demand comes from our Creator.

V. The Ten Commandments each build on and protect an important and fragile dimension of the creation order.

Each of the commandments makes certain assumptions about human life and the created moral order. Because of the reality of this created order, it is possible for people to abuse this order or go the wrong direction within this order. Some examples will make this clear.

We are commanded, "You shall not bear false witness against your neighbor." A crucial assumption of this commandment is that words are powerful and play a large role in relationships and in society. This is a distinct dimension or structure of the created moral order. Part of the image of God in us is that our words make things happen; after all, God created the whole universe by speaking. We also create by means of words, including plans, policies, goals, reports, and even the words we speak only to ourselves. Of course, relationships are created largely by means of words. And everything we create by means of words can also be destroyed by means of words. The verbal structure of human life is fragile. This is enough on the topic of speech to illustrate the way this commandment builds on and protects a particular dimension of the created moral order. Or maybe we should say the commandment requires us to go in the right direction within a created structure.

A second illustration using a different commandment may be in order. We are told in the first commandment, "You shall have no other gods before me." Of course, this commandment confronts idolatry, which is common. This commandment is necessary because of at least two dimensions of the created moral order. First, people are incurably religious. Even if people do not worship the true God, they can hardly stop themselves from looking somewhere for their hope, comfort, and meaning. And as soon as people turn somewhere for hope and comfort, they turn something created, some created good, into a God-substitute, hoping this idol will provide what they need. This dimension of human life moved the atheist philosopher Ludwig Feuerbach to say that the main difference between humans and animals is that people are religious. Idolatry would not be possible as a sin if people were not created as religious beings. This first commandment builds on and directs this dimension of the created moral order.

The first commandment also builds on and directs a second dimension of the created moral order. This has to do with the role of religion in personal and cultural life. False religion, idolatry, is important not only because it insults God but also because religion plays such a large role in shaping personal and cultural life. If we worship personal peace and affluence, our lives will take one shape; if we worship our Creator and Redeemer, our lives will take another shape. The philosopher Paul Tillich summarized some of the better sociological and anthropological insights when he said, "Culture is the form of religion; religion is the substance of culture." This observation may not be as penetrating and critical as the Old Testament assessment of why idolatry is so dreadful. About idols we read, "Those who make them will be like them, and so will all who trust in them." (Psalm 135:18) The first commandment builds on a crucial dimension of how God created human life: Our choice of an object of worship will play a massive role in shaping our personal and cultural life. This relationship between worship and the shape of human life is part of the creation order.

These comments on two of the commandments must be seen as illustrative of a principle of interpretation. Each of the ten builds on, protects, and directs our actions in relation to a particular dimension or structure of the created order that is at risk because of sin. Some parts of the creation order, such as the law of gravity, are not fragile. We cannot easily break them. But other parts of the creation order are fragile and easily destroyed by sin. The commandments teach us how to use the different dimensions of creation properly and how to move in the right direction within the various structures of creation.

VI. The Ten Commandments were given to us in a particular organic order.

The Decalogue does not begin with the prohibition of adultery, nor does it end with the rule against lying. Even if you have not thought about it, you probably sense a certain order of presentation. Some reflection on this order can teach us much about moral life and experience. The first commandment addresses the deepest motives of our hearts, the choice of an object for our worship. This commandment seems to be in the first position because all of life flows from our choice of an object of worship. With a little exaggeration, one might say that our response to the first commandment determines our response to the other commandments. The second and third commandments build on the basic principles of the first commandment, giving much more definition and content to our worship while also speaking to the problems of our worship becoming mixed with idolatry or unbalanced from an improper view of God. The fourth commandment (Sabbath) requires that our worship include the public institutional expression of our faith. It is not only about a day but also about public worship, which requires having a time, a place, a plan, facilities, and so on. It is valuable to see that the Sabbath commandment stands between the commandments that may be largely hidden matters of the heart (the first three) and the commandments that address public social matters such as stealing, lying, and murder. This order closely parallels an important characteristic of life: a person's faith begins to effectively transform his life partly by means of participation in public worship with a worshipping community. People can claim to have a deep faith without that faith having much effect on their life and habits. Participation in worship, Bible study, prayer, giving, serving, and witnessing in a real community with a living congregation turns a hidden faith into a transformed life. The fourth commandment makes a hidden faith public and equips a person for the commands that follow.

The fifth commandment, concerning honoring parents, is in some ways similar to the Sabbath command. People who have intact relations with their parents and who also keep the Sabbath will be largely equipped to keep the following commandments. Phrased differently, it is by means of church and family that a real faith becomes a power that changes life and culture. And even those people who do not share in the life of faith in the church, but who do have intact relations with their parents, are much better able to keep the following commandments and have a humane life in society. Even without a proper faith, an intact family is a means of common grace that helps keep human life humane.

Commandments six through nine are the primary social commandments. They are intended to protect life, marriage, property, and truth. Though most societies have some rules on these topics because these topics are central to the natural moral law (revealed by God through creation), these commandments remind us that God is very interested in these matters. Our actions in all these areas are either glorifying or dishonoring to God. They are the major areas of concern in the study of applied ethics.

The last commandment says, "You shall not covet." As the apostle Paul discovered (Romans 7:7), this is a commandment that is different from the previous four. We cannot easily deceive ourselves into thinking we have fulfilled it. All of us covet in some way at some time. But coveting is not really a specific sin as much as it is a desire to commit some other sinful action. The commandment says we are not to covet a neighbor's house or wife, referring back to the commandments about stealing and adultery, in this way illustrating God's expectation of a right attitude or desire in relation to all the commandments. So the last commandment is a principle of interpreting all the commandments: all the commandments require not only the right actions but also the right desires and intentions. All the commandments address the attitudes of the human heart.

If we encounter the last commandment properly, it forces us to our knees to confess our sin, and then it drives us back to the beginning of the Decalogue, to learn that our God is a God who delivers from bondage. This means that the order of the commandments is not exactly a line; it is more like a circle. Once we have discovered that our hearts are filled with coveting, then we are ready to properly consider the question of a pure faith, which is demanded by the first three commandments.

VII. The Commandments contain a dynamic dialogue between law and grace.

Throughout the Bible we are confronted by both the gospel, a set of promises of God's grace, and the law, which is a set of commands to obey. For the life of faith to stay in balance, we must be continually responding to both the law and the gospel. Distortions arise when either is neglected or misconstrued. What we might miss is the way in which the Decalogue itself points to the life of faith as a dynamic dialogue with both the law and the gospel.

Of course the Ten Commandments are primarily law, the outline of all of God's law. Where do we see the gospel of grace in the Decalogue? The first place is the preamble: "I am the Lord your God who brought you out of Egypt, out of the land of slavery." For Old Testament believers, the Exodus out of Egypt was the great act of God to rescue and save them. In their faith, the Exodus played a role very similar to the role played by the death and resurrection of Jesus for New Testament believers. It was the key historical event which formed a basis for their redemption, faith, and identity. As New Testament believers, we could almost substitute a preamble that says something like, "I am the Lord your God who sent Jesus to pay for all your sins." Of course this sets the Ten Commandments into a context or framework of a life of response to God's grace and gospel, a life of gratitude. It would be a monumental mistake for us to neglect reading the preamble when we read the Decalogue.

A second place we see the dynamic dialogue between law and gospel is in the third commandment, "You shall not misuse the name of the Lord your God." In parts of the Old Testament, and especially in the book of Exodus, the phrase "name of God" had a very particular meaning. It referred to a proper recognition of both God's holiness and wrath, on the one hand, but also his grace and mercy, on the other hand. In Exodus 34: 6, 7 God proclaimed his own name to Moses saying, "The Lord, the Lord, the compassionate and gracious God, slow to anger, abounding in love and faithfulness, maintaining love to thousands, and forgiving wickedness, rebellion, and sin. Yet he does not leave the guilty unpunished; he punishes the children and their children for the sin of the fathers to the third and fourth generation."

This description of God explains what his "name" means: the carefully balanced understanding of both God's grace and his wrath on sin. In this balanced description of God, we see the basis for both the promise of forgiveness in the gospel and the demand for obedience to his law. To not misuse the name of God, to speak of him properly, requires we that keep both his law and his gospel, with his wrath and his grace in view.

A final way we see the dialogue between law and gospel is in the last commandment. When God says, "You shall not covet," all we can do is fall to our knees and say, "God, be merciful to me, a sinner." If we are honest with ourselves, God's law will drive us to seek his grace and forgiveness once again.

VIII. Reflections

God's law will probably always be controversial among fallen men and women. People love or hate God's commands, and maybe both at the same time. This complex reaction is to be expected because the law both confronts our sinfulness and guides us in the direction of living consistently with how God created us to live. In the midst of these strong feelings, and maybe to overcome these strong feelings, it is important to interpret the commandments carefully. It is certainly wise to always emphasize that the law is not the gospel and is not the way to earn salvation, since mistakes on this topic are so common and so serious. It is also certainly wise to emphasize that the commandments fit so closely with the general revelation of the natural moral law and with the created moral order. This helps overcome the misunderstanding that sees God's law as arbitrary or destructive of human well-being. These insights can help us learn to love God's law. And once we begin to love God's law, understanding its multiple valuable roles in our lives, we should want to give God's law its proper place in our lives. Perhaps posting the Ten Commandments on government buildings is no longer wise or possible in some parts of the world, but making regular use of God's law in all our churches and Christian ministries should be an organic part of our response to the moral relativism of our age. Christians do not need to the removal of God's law from public life by removing God's law from the church, the family, and private schools. And so long as the law is understood in proper relation to the gospel of Christ, it will continue to address the most dynamic existential conflicts of the human heart.

Further reading on the Ten Commandments

There are two truly classical studies in the special hermeneutics of the Decalogue that theological students will surely want to read. They are John Calvin, *Institutes of the Christian Religion*, Book II, Chapter 8, sections 1 to 12 (Final Latin version in 1559, translated by Ford Lewis Battles, edited by John T. McNeill, Philadelphia: The Westminster Press, 1960); and Charles Hodge, *Systematic Theology*, Vol. 3, Chapter 19, sections 1 to 3 (originally published in 1873. Reprint edition, Grand Rapids: Wm. B. Eerdmans, 1986.) An excellent overview of Calvin and classical Reformed theology related to the law is I. John Hesselink, *Calvin's Concept of the Law* (Allison Park, PA: Pickwick Publications, 1992).

The distinction between law and gospel was classically developed for evangelical thought by Martin Luther, especially in his *Commentary on Galatians* of 1536, which is available in various editions. The connection between natural law and the Decalogue was classically articulated by Thomas Aquinas in his *Treatise on Law,* which is questions 90–97 of his *Summa Theologica*, originally published in the 1270s, now available in various editions. The views of Aquinas were substantially followed by Calvin and Luther and can bear the type of light improvement suggested by Albert Wolters in *Creation Regained* (Grand Rapids: Wm. B. Eerdmans, 1985).

The slogan "The war of all against all" was probably coined by Thomas Hobbes and enjoys a prominent place in his work *Leviathan* (1651). Good excerpts from Hobbes are found in most good anthologies of readings in ethics and political theory. Ludwig Feuerbach's philosophy of religion received its most prominent articulation in his *Essence of Christianity* (1841), selections of which are found in many good anthologies on the history of philosophy. The Tillich quotation is from "Aspects of a Religious

Analysis of Culture," in *Theology of Culture* by Paul Tillich (Oxford University Press, 1959).

Chapter VIII: Biblical Principles in the Public Square

Theological Foundations for Christian Civic Participation

A few years ago I had the privilege of presenting a special lecture at a Czech government conference on family policy.[98] In this special lecture I argued that certain foundational values are extremely important because they should shape the actions of government, family, and business in relation to children. I claimed that responsible people should make certain value decisions which will lead to a series of actions, feelings, and reactions in personal relationships, government policy, and business planning. These value decisions include seeing children fundamentally as gifts, not as problems; deciding to practice family loyalty, meaning not abandoning one's children or spouse; and consciously trying to practice a combination of unconditional love and structured justice, which should be a human reflection or image of the combination of God's grace and God's law.

In this special lecture I decided not to initially emphasize the fact that I am a Christian and an evangelical pastor, but this was not a cowardly effort to hide my core identity and belief structure. I was there in the role of a moral philosopher who has something significant to contribute to the discussion of values and family life, regardless of the religion or beliefs of each of the people at the conference. But what I said was very consciously shaped by a set of evangelical theological beliefs that should, I think, inform the participation of Christians in discussions of values and moral principles in the public square. My philosophy, including my philosophy of family values and public life, is self-consciously a result of my theology; this is not the result of me being some type of religious fanatic; it is a normal but often unrecognized part of the human condition that our ultimate beliefs about the nature of the universe exercise extensive influence over our penultimate or secondary beliefs and convictions in the everyday realms of family, child raising, education, and public policy. I would hope that my ultimate convictions slowly became clear to some of the people

---

[98] This was an international conference on family policy hosted by the Czech Ministry of Labor and Social Affairs and held on November 22, 2007, in Prague reprinted in chapter 3 of this book.

who heard my lecture, though many people at the conference may not have perceived the deeper principles that underlie what I said. While I did not initially emphasize my Christian faith in this lecture, I did not leave my faith at home; I was practicing what I would call an indirect or implicit apology for the Christian faith.

The theological principles which guided this lecture on family values are, I believe, worthy of clarification for other Christians who are called to active participation in the public discussion of values and moral principles. In this essay, I am inviting the reader to join me in the theological research laboratory, to consider some deep background theological convictions that led me to this manner of cultural and political engagement.

In a certain sense, all Christians are called to engagement with "the world," the whole pattern of cultures in partial rebellion against God, because Jesus wants us to be "in the world" but not "of the world." Jesus did not ask us to somehow leave or withdraw from the world, which would probably be impossible, since the sin, unbelief, pride, and ingratitude which make "the world" so objectionable to God reside deep within us. We cannot withdraw from "the world," because we tend to take the world with us wherever we go. But Jesus warned us seriously not to be conformed to the world as it is, since our world is so deeply influenced by sin and misbelief. Unless we are in a situation of serious persecution, a "fight or flight" relation to society is probably not wise. We should see ourselves as sent by God into the world as people who both hear and carry God's Word of law and gospel. Once we see ourselves in this way, we will begin to understand that our Christian faith has a multi-faceted relation to the many cultures in which we live and in which we both hear and proclaim the biblical message.

One of the relations of the biblical message to any culture is that of contributing to that culture in the realm of moral values and ethical principles. Many of the better characteristics of several cultures around the world are partly the result of 2000 years of history during which many biblical values and principles have been given to those cultures. Christians have not only cared for the helpless, freed the slaves, and fed the poor; believers have also articulated their moral reasons for doing these sorts of things, and these moral reasons have often become a gift from the Body of Christ to the rest of the culture, thereby making decisive contributions to the moral reasoning and practice of multiple cultures around the world. In light of this distinguished history, we, as Christians, should learn how to articulate our central moral beliefs more effectively within the public square so that we consciously contribute to and influence public action, policies, and attitudes; in addition to influencing our cultures, this type of effort should also render many of our biblically influenced moral concerns more understandable to our non-believing neighbors, perhaps reducing their resistance to the gospel of salvation in Christ. Learning to publicly articulate our central moral convictions should be an educational priority for believers serving in education or church leadership, but it should also be seen as important for believers serving in business leadership or in government. For the glory of God and for the good of our communities, there are some things we need to learn. This essay is an introduction to this field of study. It will be outlined around a series of theological/ethical principles that can inform our participation in public discussions of values and moral principles.

I. People generally know more about right and wrong than they will initially admit to knowing.

In Romans 1:32 the apostle Paul made an astonishing claim about moral knowledge. After listing a whole set of inappropriate behaviors, such as envy, murder, slander, deceit, and gossip, he said, "Although they know God's righteous decree that those who do such things deserve death, they not only continue to do these very things but also approve of those who practice them." The profundity of his thought requires reflection. He claims that people generally truly know a tremendous amount about right and wrong, and this knowledge is true knowledge that comes from God, but at the same time, in an act of terrible self-contradiction, these same people will approve the actions they know to be wrong and talk as if they do not know that these actions are wrong. This is part of the self-deceiving self-contradiction of the unbeliever. On the one hand, he/she cannot carry on everyday life without knowing a certain amount about right and wrong, for all of our everyday interactions with other people assume we all know we should not murder, lie, and steal; and by means of his general revelation, God provides enough moral knowledge to all people so that people have the moral knowledge needed for everyday life. But on the other hand, such moral knowledge is terrifying, since it is not simply moral information about how to treat other people; it is also the knowledge that our common failure to follow the moral law deserves God's condemnation.

This situation puts tremendous spiritual stress on the unbeliever, and this spiritual stress leads to a number of different self deceiving intellectual moves, unless the person is willing to fall before God and cry, "God, be merciful to me, a sinner." By calling these moves "intellectual" I am not implying that this is somehow the sort of thing most normally done by scholars and philosophers; taxi drivers and factory workers probably think the same things as professors and school teachers, while using a different vocabulary. I call them "intellectual moves" because they have to do with ways of thinking.

One of the most common of these intellectual moves in our time is moral relativism, which simply denies that there is any real moral law and therefore claims there is no objective right and wrong. Any feelings about right and wrong, it is said, are only related (in this sense, relative) to a particular person or culture, and therefore they are not based on any universal moral law. It is worth observing that while our philosophy can be relativistic, life is not relativistic. There are moral norms which we encounter everyday in every relationship. Even the man with a strongly relativistic philosophy may not talk like a relativist if you steal his car or sleep with his wife. And without doing anything so stupid, there are things one can say or do to help people break out of their moral relativism. The main point here is that moral relativism is one common intellectual move in reaction to the spiritual stress of knowing (but not wanting to know) that breaking God's law deserves God's wrath.

A second common intellectual move to avoid this stress is the secularization of ethics. Since the Enlightenment it has been very common to think of ethics as having nothing to do with God. Some moral theories have said ethics is simply a matter of our rational duty; others say ethics is a matter of the social contract, the formal or informal agreements which hold society together in good order; many say ethics is simply a matter of what actions or policies lead to good results for people; and today is it popular to say that ethics has to do with reaching human potential. There is a valuable element of truth in each of these theories, but what is common to them all is to neglect any relation between the moral law and God. Each of these common moral theories allows people to talk about right and wrong while pretending to forget God's decree that people who do certain things deserve death. Such moral theories may truly help people to be good citizens and good neighbors, practicing a kind of active, civil righteousness (called "Righteousness No. 1" below), but at the same time such theories seem to be a way to reduce spiritual stress by saying people know less about right and wrong than they really do.

A third common intellectual move to reduce moral/spiritual stress is to try to reduce our recognition of our moral obligations before God to something we can claim to follow. The ethical maxim, "If I should, then I can," is an expression of a heart and mind that does not want to recognize the depths of God's demand on our lives. If people deceive themselves into thinking they have followed whatever moral demands they encounter, then they also may convince themselves they do not deserve death, if God does happen to exist. The attempt to substantially reduce the moral demand which we all face is a common human phenomenon. It is part of the attempt to reduce spiritual stress without asking for God's forgiveness.

In all discussions of fundamental moral values and principles in the public square, Christians need to be aware of the conflicted nature of moral knowledge among unbelievers. The problem is not entirely that they lack moral information. The problem is spiritual stress which results from knowing more about God's demand and God's law than they want to know; this stress often leads to a range of intellectual moves or mental tricks to reduce moral/spiritual stress which make such discussions very complicated.

II. There is harmony between the content of God's special revelation and God's general revelation.

We call the Bible God's special revelation, meaning those promises and that information which God made known to believers in a special way over the centuries and which has been faithfully preserved for our benefit in written form in the Scriptures. In contrast, God's general revelation is his "speech" through the entirety of his creation (which includes human reason and feelings which reflect the image of God). There are significant differences between the two forms of revelation, both in terms of content and in terms of means of human learning. The Bible, God's special revelation, does not provide detailed information about plant genetics or the characteristics of the various planets; for that detailed information I must rely on the general revelation of truth from God through his creation which is perceived and organized by natural science. And general revelation in creation does not tell me very much, if anything, about God's offer of forgiveness in Christ; for that information I must rely on the special revelation of truth from God which comes to us through the Bible. Obviously we make many mistakes in our attempts to understand both general revelation and special revelation, but if we understand both correctly, they will agree, since both convey truth that comes from God. Ultimately, all truth comes from God, and truth is God's opinion on a question. There will be no final conflict between a properly understood general revelation and a properly understood special revelation; but to say there is no *final* conflict between a properly understood general revelation and a properly understood special revelation implies there may be many *intermediate* conflicts between our understandings of general and special revelation, some of which will be mistaken.

The moral law occupies a somewhat strange position because *both* general revelation *and* special revelation constantly present us with the demands of God's law. When I read the Bible, I am very directly confronted with God's commands. But when I pay any significant attention to human experience and human relationships, I am also confronted with moral demands which the believer can recognize to be God's demands, as they come to me via his general revelation. Many areas of knowledge deal either mostly with general revelation or mostly with special revelation. A book on the meaning of the cross of Christ will be properly focused on special revelation, whereas a book on the proper use of a medical diagnostic technique might properly only use God's general revelation. But a comprehensive book on ethics and moral knowledge will have to analyze knowledge we receive both via general revelation and special revelation, because God's moral law is extensively revealed in both modes of revelation. For that reason, scholars in the study of Christian ethics might also be philosophers or sociologists as well as students of the Bible, and they cannot stop considering questions of the interconnections of faith and different types of learning.

In our time in the post-Christian West it is the demands of God's law as it comes to us through God's general revelation that many people prefer to ignore, since most of our neighbors have little, if any, contact with biblical revelation. Even people who claim to be Christians often have very little effective contact with the biblical revelation. This fact should inform how we talk about God's law within our secular society. We should regularly mention the multifaceted character of our moral knowledge. For example, I know that my wife and children need real loyalty from me, and this knowledge comes from the relationships as well as from the Bible. I know that my colleagues need real honesty from me, and this moral demand comes from those relationships as well as from the Bible. I know that my neighbors should expect justice from me, and this knowledge comes from civic relationships as well as from the Bible. As a believer, my moral knowledge is a complete unity of what I have learned through both general and special revelation. But my non-Christian neighbors have some of the same knowledge, which they have received via God's general revelation. But that knowledge is not completed, confirmed, and reformulated by means of God's special revelation, which would also change partly rejected knowledge into fully accepted knowledge.

For this reason, when people read the moral commands of God in the Bible, commands like "you shall not steal; you shall murder; you shall not commit adultery," they do not exactly receive new information. They hear in explicit written and oral form what they probably already knew, though their previous knowledge may have been less well-clarified and perhaps partly rejected. The moral law which comes from God has a prominent place in both general and special revelation. If properly understood, there will be harmony between our understanding of the moral demands in both general and special revelation, since the moral law comes from God, though it reaches us in two ways. For many believers, this harmony of the two ways of encountering the moral law is so deep and uniform that they rarely observe that we encounter God's law in two ways.

This harmony does not in any way make the special revelation of God's law less important. As mentioned, there is extreme value in having his law written on stone in a public manner. And the special revelation of God's law always sets his law in close contact with the various promises of God and especially the gospel of God's grace in Christ; this changes everything about our relationship with the moral law. In the most profound possible way, the special revelation of God's law (with the revelation of his grace in Christ) renews our previous knowledge of his law which came via general revelation. In the terms used by older theology, "grace restores nature;" in my terminology, the special revelation of God's moral law restores our broken understanding of the moral law which we previously received via his general revelation. But this does not eliminate the importance of understanding the way in which God is still revealing his moral law through creation to all people.

This harmony between the two forms of revelation of God's law is crucial background for public discussions of moral values and principles. Our neighbors who are not Christians may not know the Bible and basic Christian doctrines, but at some deep level they will normally have some awareness of the fact of a moral demand, and they will probably have some awareness of the content of that moral demand. And like it or not, they will probably be bothered by the feeling that these demands come from God. The central content of biblical moral demands will often be partly present in their minds and hearts, even if they do not like it. And in a cultural context that is consciously post-Christian, our neighbors may have deeply troubled or conflicted feelings about the entire Christian tradition which are connected with their troubled relationship with the general revelation of God's moral law.

III. We should distinguish among the different uses of God's moral law.

Historically, Protestants have distinguished among different uses or functions of God's moral law in the lives of people. Without going into this rich
history, we can note that three functions or uses of God's moral law have
received prominent attention from classical Protestant moral writers. Both
the general revelation of God's law and the special revelation of God's
moral law have these three uses. They are: 1. the theological or condemn-
ing/convicting use of God's law; 2. the civil or political use of God's moral
law; and 3. the moral law of God as a guide for the Christian life of gratitude.

The theological or condemning use of God's law has to do with our
awareness of our sin and guilt before God. "Through the law we become
conscious of sin." (Romans 3:20) By means of the moral law, we become
aware that we are sinners before a holy God, and in this sense, it is by
means of the moral law that we get to know ourselves. Maybe the law says,
"You shall not covet," and we recognize that we constantly covet. Maybe
the law says, "You shall not steal," and we recognize ourselves as thieves.
Or maybe the entire law prompts a reaction in us, so that we have to recognize that sometimes we want things and do things simply because they are
wrong. Then we are pushed by the law to see our need for forgiveness in
Christ. The law pushes us to see our need for the gospel and cry out for
God's mercy. And this occurs not only at the beginning of the life of faith,
when we first believe the gospel; this relation to the law in its condemning
function continues through a lifetime of faith, pushing us to repeatedly re-
new our trust in the gospel of Christ. Some churches make this process of
recognizing our sin and rehearing the gospel an important part of weekly
worship. As long as we have any sinful tendencies remaining, we need
God's moral law to condemn and convict us, to drive us again to trust in
the gospel. In this sense, the law always condemns.

The second use of the law has sometimes been forgotten. The moral
law has the possibility of restraining sin to the point of making a largely
humane life in society possible. This is called the civil or political or civilizing function of God's moral law. Why is it that most people do not usually freely follow all of their worst instincts? Why is it that much of the
world enjoys the great benefit of civilized life together, even though our
sinful nature can so easily lead to the "war of all against all?" People do
not usually become as terrible as they might possibly become because of
some type of moral restraint. This moral restraint will often be complex in

nature, partly consisting of cultural expectations and government laws, partly consisting in habits learned at home, school, or work, partly consisting in moral principles, rules, and values. God's law is built into creation in such a way that it is an unavoidable part of the creation order, even if people do not like it, claim not to know that a moral law exists, and claim to be atheists. And even if people reduce the demands of God's law to the point that it is something easy to follow, this vastly reduced or twisted moral understanding generally has a positive and civilizing effect in human life. It makes a partly humane civilization possible. Even if the moral law in this civil or civilizing function does not reflect God's moral law with 100% purity, it may still be enough to significantly improve the behavior of individuals and an entire society.

Believers should not only be aware of the way in which God's law in its civilizing function influences us; we also need to become very conscious of the way in which the Body of Christ is one of God's means of making his law effective within a particular culture. For 2000 years Christians have contributed a wide range of biblically informed moral values, principles, examples, and theories to many different cultures; this has had a profound effect on what people regard as proper and civilized behavior. Something similar happened through God's Jewish people in the time before the birth of the Christian church. Awareness of these historical facts should influence our understanding of the calling of the Body of Christ in society today.

The third use of the moral law is that of providing a guide for believers for how to live a life of gratitude to God for his gifts of creation and salvation. The person who is justified before God by faith, who is aware of forgiveness and a new status as an adopted child of God, faces the important question, "How do I properly show my gratitude to God?" At least part of the answer is to follow God's commands as we receive them in the Bible and in general revelation. For example, instead of desiring to kill, steal, lie, or commit adultery, I must really want to protect life, protect assets, protect truth, and protect marriage and turn these renewed desires into actions as part of a life of gratitude to God for his gifts of life and grace. In this way, the law of God plays an important role in the authentically Christian life, the life of faith; the moral law of God is part of the core structure of the life of gratitude.

What we must not miss is my claim that it is the same moral law of God, encountered in both general and special revelation, which is used in all the uses of God's law. This means that there is a large degree of similarity between actions resulting from the civilizing use of the law and the use of God's law as a guide to gratitude. A person who is an atheist or agnostic may be very careful to tell the truth very consistently, and his/her explanation of that action may be something like, "We have a rational duty to tell the truth," or "If I ever say anything false, no one will trust me." These are partial but good explanations of why truth telling is important which arise from the way God's moral law is built into human life and experience. In this way, the general revelation of God's law pushes people toward a more humane and civilized way of life, showing the effectiveness of the civilizing use of God's moral law. Another person who is a serious Christian also is very serious about consistently telling the truth, and his/her explanation of that action may be something like "Truth telling glorifies God because God is truthful," or "Truth telling shows my gratitude to God, because he commands truthfulness." For this person, the special revelation of God's law provides guidance for the life of gratitude, which we numbered the third use of God's law. In terms of the outward action, there will be a very significant similarity between the actions of the two people, that of truth telling, while there will simultaneously be a huge element of difference regarding internal meaning and motivation. In this case, the atheist is trying to be a good person, neighbor, and citizen, whereas the believer is trying to glorify God in gratitude for his gifts, which should also lead to being a good neighbor and a good citizen.

IV. There is compatibility and difference among the different types of righteousness.

Since the time of Martin Luther, it has been common for Protestants to distinguish different types of righteousness, for example the difference between the active righteousness of following God's law and the passive righteousness which comes by faith in the promise of the gospel. This distinction was sometimes described as a contrast between civil righteousness and spiritual righteousness, though that way of talking might lead some to the problem of thinking that faith and civic affairs have little or nothing in common. For that reason, it is probably better not to make a strong contrast between civic and spiritual righteousness an important part of our thinking.

In the discussion of ethics in the public square, we should make a distinction between two types of righteousness, both of which are active and civic though they have very different motivations and spiritual directions. Finding good terminology may be difficult. Righteousness number 1, in this distinction, is being a good neighbor and a good citizen because of a partly positive response to the general revelation of God's law, partly because of other ways in which biblical moral principles have been included within a culture or a person's self-expectations. This person might deny that the moral law comes from God or claim to be uncertain about this question; he or she might significantly reduce what the moral law demands so that it is far easier to fulfill; this person may articulate an ethical theory that seems insufficient; and yet this person may be a good citizen and a good neighbor. Righteousness number 2, in this distinction, is attempting to "do justice, love mercy, and walk humbly with God" in conscious, believing response to God's gifts of creation and redemption. This person wants to genuinely love God and his neighbors in obedience to all of God's commands, motivated by gratitude for God's grace, with a heart filled with faith in all of God's promises. This is the difference between a somewhat positive response to God's law in its civilizing use and the completely positive response to both the gospel and the special revelation of God's law. This strange terminology, Righteousness 1 and Righteousness 2, is intended to show both the significant similarity and the radical difference between these two types of active, civic righteousness.

The similarities between Righteousness No. 1 and Righteousness No. 2: in practice, the two types of righteousness will include very similar actions, as described above in the illustration of truth telling. Both of these types of active, civic-minded righteousness will include honesty, loyalty, mercy, and a deep concern for fairness or justice. Both types of righteousness should include a real concern for matters of the common good, including economic, political, medical, environmental, and educational concerns. Both types of active righteousness should include real concern for many family values, including love for children and loyalty to one's spouse. Both types of righteousness are radically different from a life of crime, negligence, irresponsibility, laziness, cruelty, dishonesty, corruption, and general delinquency. Both types of active righteousness would lead to real improvements in the everyday world and contribute to justice, peace, and mercy.

But we must not minimize the radical differences between these two types of righteousness. Somewhere Augustine observes that the virtues of the pagans are glorious vices. By this he probably meant that the virtues of the pagans, which I have called "Righteousness No. 1," are ultimately motivated by love of self, not love of God. A really smart person will not love himself by a life of crime and obvious vice; a really smart person may love himself and give full expression to his arrogant pride by a life of seemingly humble public service for the common good. This is a truly glorious vice.

Martin Luther observed that there is deep in the human heart a desire to justify ourselves before God, in effect to tell God that the gospel of Christ is not needed, since we can justify or cleanse ourselves; and this desire, Luther thought, is mixed into all our normal "rational" considerations of the moral demands built into creation. Of course, he thought, it is much better for our life in society to be governed by the rational consideration of good laws and principles than for our life in society to be governed by irrational passions like revenge, prejudice, or greed. And this is possible, Luther thought, because God has built his moral law into creation and into human reason. But this type of active righteousness, which I have called Righteousness No. 1, may sometimes promote the most fundamental of all theological mistakes, that of thinking we can earn our salvation before God, so that the gospel of Christ is not needed.

In our time, we can easily observe another deep weakness in most common varieties of Righteousness No. 1. Our world is filled with a whirlwind of competing ideologies, religions, and worldviews, many of which contain ideas which substantially reduce or twist the perception of the moral law which God built into creation and reason. Whether it is an ideology that says the unborn or the disabled are not human, that says marriage is not important, or that gives a strange religious justification for murder or lying, the minds of people are filled with ideas and beliefs that make it more difficult for them to respond positively to the general revelation of God's moral law. This leads to the religious or philosophical attempts to justify actions that seem totally repugnant in light of the biblical revelation, e.g., abortion, easy divorce, cohabitation, temporary marriages, jihad, and deception. The biblical revelation needs to play an important role in our moral thinking to help us avoid the various types of religious and philosophical deception that so easily cloud the moral thinking of many. Without the influence of special revelation, Righteousness No. 1 can very easily go astray.

V. Both Common Grace and Special Grace Are Truly Grace.

It has long been the practice for evangelical Christians to distinguish between two types of grace which come from God, his common grace and his special grace. Special grace has to do with salvation, eternal life, and the forgiveness of sins. Common grace has to do with all those things that make life in this world possible. A favorite biblical explanation of common grace is in the Sermon on the Mount. Jesus taught us, "Love your enemies and pray for those who persecute you, that you may be sons of our Father in heaven. He causes his sun to rise on the evil and the good, and sends rain on the righteous and the unrighteous." (Matthew 5: 44, 45) Our love for our enemies should image or reflect our Father's love for his enemies, to whom he graciously provides those things needed for daily life. Since we need some good way to describe this work of God, why not call it "common grace?"

On God's side, this common grace is part of his call to repentance. In his evangelistic sermon in Lystra, the apostle Paul claimed God "has not left himself without testimony: He has shown kindness by giving you rain from heaven and crops in their seasons; he provides you with plenty of food and fills your hearts with joy." (Acts 14:17) And in Romans 2:4, Paul completed the thought: "Do you show contempt for the riches of his kindness, not realizing that God's kindness leads you toward repentance?" The kindness of God, joined with the human appreciation of the kindness of God, should lead people to repentance and faith.

This common grace of God stands in relationship to the common wrath of God. (The common wrath of God should be contrasted with multiple types of particular wrath, as well as contrasted with the eschatological wrath of God, each of which we see described in the Bible in different places. God's wrath is always truly just and is never arbitrary. It is displayed in several ways.) The biblical description of the wrath of God which I have most seriously studied is that in Romans 1:18-32. Of course, there is much biblical teaching about the wrath of God that does not appear within this text. What is striking in this text is the way in which the common wrath of God is depicted. The major theme of this text is that of the current revelation of the wrath of God within history. Paul writes, "The wrath of God is being revealed." His language points to an ongoing, current work of God's wrath in the world. And at three points in the following paragraphs he describes this wrath in greater detail. In verse 24 he says, "God gave them over in the sinful desires of their hearts." In verse 26 he says, "God gave them over to shameful lusts." And in verse 28 he says, "He gave them over to a depraved mind." In each of these three statements, the wrath of God is demonstrated by letting people become more sinful in action. It is an act of God's wrath when he lets people follow more of the sinful desires within their sinful hearts.

It is not explicitly stated in this text, but it would strongly seem to follow that one of the works of God's common grace, in strict contrast with this work of his common wrath, is to restrain sin. When the sinful tendencies of a person or a culture are restrained, we should thank God; and then we should probably remember that this restraint of sin is a work of God's common grace, regardless of what secondary means God has used to bring about such a restraint of sin. And the common grace of God is intended to lead people to repentance and faith. Without the restraint of human evil, society can easily degenerate into the war of all against all so that an entire society self-destructs. The restraint of human self-destruction is as much a work of God's common grace as is the sending of rain and sun.

Such a restraint of sin will often result in what I called Righteousness No. 1. The person who benefits from such sin-restraining common grace might still profess ideas and be motivated by desires that are not God-honoring. But whatever cultural, religious, personal, political, or economic motives are involved, it is by God's common grace that people restrain sin and practice any type of righteousness. This common grace of God was assumed by the Apostle Paul in his noted description of human governments in Romans 13. He wrote, "Everyone must submit himself to the governing authorities, for there is no authority except that which God has established. The authorities that exist have been established by God. ... (The person in authority) is God's servant to do you good. But if you do wrong, be afraid, for he does not bear the sword for nothing. He is God's servant, an agent of wrath to bring punishment on the wrongdoer. ... This is also why you pay taxes, for the authorities are God's servants." (Romans 13:1-6)

By putting a restraint on some of the more destructive sins, the civil authorities are a means of God's common grace. For that we must be thankful to God and to them by means of doing our part, by practicing our civic duties and paying our taxes. Good civil government is an important means of God's common grace. To make this truth vivid in our minds we only need to contrast pictures of genocide or violent rioting in the streets with pictures of peaceful argument in a parliament, legislature, or court of law.

By using the word "grace" to describe the gifts of God such as rain, sun, and a peaceful life in society, Christians have recognized that these are undeserved gifts of God. It is common to emphasize that God's special grace of salvation in Christ, forgiveness of sins, and justification before God by faith arise from God's grace, his undeserved love and mercy. Those gifts we call common grace are just as much a result of God's grace as those gifts we call special grace. Those gifts of God that make a civilized, peaceful, satisfying daily life possible are as truly the result of God's undeserved love and grace as are the gifts of salvation and forgiveness. But the gifts are very different, so we should distinguish between common grace and special grace.

VI. Christians Are Called to Be Servants of Both Special Grace and Common Grace.

Jesus said, "Go and make disciples of all nations." (Matthew 28:19) This is the missions mandate or Great Commission; based in Jesus' claim of authority over all peoples and cultures, it has empowered believers with the conviction of the universal importance and relevance of the biblical message. It is a call for believers to become servants of God's special grace.

The call of God to be servants of special grace is connected with God's call to believers to be servants of common grace. In the parable of "The Sheep and the Goats" Jesus taught us, "Then the King will say to those on his right, 'Come, you who are blessed by my Father; take your inheritance, the kingdom prepared for you since the creation of the world. For I was hungry and you gave me something to eat, I was thirsty and you gave me something to drink, I was a stranger and you invited me in, I needed clothes, and you clothed me, I was in prison and you came to visit me.' Then the righteous will answer him, 'Lord, when did we see you hungry and feed you, or thirsty and give you something to drink? When did we see you a stranger and invite you in, or needing clothes and clothe you? When did we see you sick or in prison and go to visit you?' The King will reply, 'I tell you the truth, whatever you did for the least of these my brothers of mine, you did for me.'" (Matthew 25:34-40)

There can hardly be a more pointed and direct call from Jesus to become imitators of and participants in God's work of common grace. He seems to evaluate our claim to be his followers by looking at whether or not we practice actions that are similar to his Father's common grace. The Father shows common grace to many of his enemies, made in his image, by giving them rain, sun, and all things needed for life in this world, including good government. He calls us to imitate, reflect, and image him by helping and taking care of the people made in the image of God. There can hardly be a more powerful motivation to become the giving hands of Jesus in relation to a world filled with suffering. Jesus calls us to be servants of his special saving grace by declaring the gospel and also to be servants of his common, humanizing and civilizing grace.

There does not seem to be a sharp line between God's common grace that sends rain and sun and God's common grace that restrains sin. Both are works of God's grace that make life possible but do not immediately lead to salvation or forgiveness of sins. In much of the world today, the need for humanitarian aid arises when the sinful tendencies within the human heart have not been restrained. Too many humanitarian crises are the result of war, violence, economic collapse caused by corruption, or illness caused partly by irresponsible behavior (Think of drug use.). These humanitarian disasters, which properly move the hearts of believers to compassionate action, have arisen partly because there had been no effective restraint of certain types of sins at an earlier time. How much more compassionate it would be to prevent such humanitarian disasters, by being servants of God's common grace at that earlier time! Or think of the many problems of children, addressed by countless educators and counselors, that arise because they were abandoned, abused, or neglected by one or both parents. Teachers and school leaders continually see children with medical, neurological, psychological, or learning problems because of the sins of the parents: e.g., alcoholism, drug abuse, father abandonment (single mothers), mother abandonment, or physical abuse. Teachers have to become something like humanitarian aid workers to help these children. How much better if the Body of Christ had effectively been served God's common grace at an earlier time, to prevent such human disasters!! If we claim to have received God' special grace, we have to become imitators of his common grace as well as proclaimers of his special grace.

VII. The Articulation of Humane Moral Values and Principles in the Public Square Is a Means of Serving God's Common Grace.

We must never forget that God's common, civilizing grace is closely connected with the moral law, whereas his special grace is more closely connected with the gospel. The restraint of sin is never perfect or complete, and this partial restraint of sin can occur when a person or a culture accepts even some parts or aspects of God's moral law. However, the restraint of sin, leading to Righteousness No. 1, will be more effective if a person's or a culture's awareness and accepted perception of the moral law are strengthened. The human perception of the moral law coming through creation is influenced by a wide variety of personal and historical factors. The public witness of the Body of Christ is one of the most important historical and personal factors that influences the common perceptions of the moral law.

One of the ways in which common grace and special grace are similar is that both are mediated partly by means of words. Protestants normally say that God's special grace is mediated to us by "The Means of Grace," the way we usually describe the combination of God's Word (including preaching and teaching in the churches, schools, and families) and the Sac-

raments (Baptism and the Holy Supper). And the Sacraments are sometimes further described as "Visible Words." In this way we emphasize the
connection of special grace to words, ultimately the word of the gospel,
without minimizing the way in which God's special grace is also mediated
by means of actions. (Obviously the gospel is a report about God's actions
in the birth, death, and resurrection of Christ, a fact which also illustrates
the connectedness between words and acts in the realm of God's special
grace.)

In God's common grace, there may be a different relationship between
words and actions. People benefit from the sun and the rain, regardless of
the words they use to describe them. But there are very significant ways in
which God's common grace is also mediated to people and cultures by
means of words.

Man does not live by bread alone. We live very extensively from our
hearts and minds, which means from words, words by which we give expression to ideas, beliefs, values, feelings, attitudes, relationships, and
much more. From the words in our minds and hearts arise very different
ways of life, for individuals and for entire cultures. The difference between
Adolph Hitler and Mother Teresa is largely what words filled their hearts
and minds. One set of words led to the Holocaust; another set of words led
to self-giving love and care for the needy. One set of words can lead to destructive totalitarianism, whereas another set of words can lead to a humane democracy. Ideas have consequences. And the set of words and ideas
shaping the life of a person or the life of a society is never entirely fixed
and unchanging. There is usually some possibility of change as a result of
what messages are communicated.

Even if people do not believe the gospel of Christ, there is real benefit
for individuals and societies if some aspects or dimensions of the total biblical message are accepted, even if that acceptance is partial. Words, slogans, sayings, mottos, theories, proverbs, and stories can all be means of
God's common grace, ways in which the Creator works in our societies to
restrain our sin and sustain a somewhat humane way of life. They can become part of the material of a humane culture, from which then arise our
feelings, our actions, and even our public policies. People who believe the
gospel of Christ and love their neighbors should jump into the very middle
of our various cultures to give voice to words, slogans, sayings, mottos,
theories, proverbs, and stories that arise from the biblical message and support the biblical message. In this way we can contribute to the cognitive,
symbolic, and emotional contents of our cultures in a way that mediates
God's common grace. Believers can contribute to the total direction of our

cultures in such a manner that more people imitate Mother Teresa and less people to walk in Hitler's footsteps. Entire societies can be encouraged and strengthened to practice higher levels of justice, honesty, loyalty, and mercy.

VIII. The Rich Complexity in God's Revelation of the Moral Law Provides and Enables a Wide Range of Methods of Presenting the Moral Law in Society.

When we pick up the Bible we see a rich complexity and complementarity in the communication of God's moral will. We find commands like "You shall not steal." We see stories or parables, like that of the Good Samaritan. We read histories, like that of the punishment of Israel for their sins. We also find a rich supply of proverbs which instruct us in the way of reflective moral wisdom. This rich pattern of communication may reach its high point in the New Testament instruction to put on the character of Christ as those who have died and risen with him. And in this rich complexity there is also real harmony, so that there is real unity in the total presentation of God's moral will. It is the self-consistent communication of a self-consistent God; therefore, the way of life of the commands fits with the way of life taught in the parables and stories, which also fits the way of life taught by the proverbs. A biblically informed virtue ethic focusing on the way of life taught in the proverbs will not be in conflict with a biblically informed rule ethic that focuses on the way of life taught by the commands; and neither will be in conflict with a way of life that arises from a biblically informed narrative ethic that focuses our attention on the proper responses to the parables and histories contained in the Bible. There is unity within complexity of communication because of the complementary character of God's special revelation.

There is the same unity within complexity in the general revelation of God's law in creation; the different dimensions of the general, creational revelation of God's law are complementary. Whether or not a person knows much about the Bible, every person in the world encounters a God-given moral demand in a wide variety of ways, some of which have been mentioned above. A few of these ways of encountering the natural moral law can be listed and described. We often have a direct, intuitive sense of what is required of us; for example a father may directly feel that his wife and children need unconditional love and complete loyalty from him, or our encounter with people experiencing pain and suffering may give us a direct moral intuition that we should practice mercy. This direct, intuitive awareness of a moral duty probably arises from our direct awareness and sense of God and his moral attributes which is partly given in general revelation and which demands that we imitate God's moral attributes because we are made in his image. Another way in which we become aware of a God-given moral demand (though perhaps without a strong awareness that the demand comes from God) is by means of thinking about predictable consequences; we might ask ourselves, "What will happen to society if everyone lies or steals?" or "What will happen to my relationships with others if I lie or steal?" This type of awareness of God's moral law arises from the way in which God has created us as relationship-oriented, while God has also built his moral law into the structure of human connectedness. Still a different way in which we become aware of a God-given moral demand is by asking what kind of person I or we are making ourselves if we take a particular action; maybe I am aware that a single impatient act or word is a step toward making me a grumpy, irritable person, which I do not want to be, whereas another action or word will tend to make me into a fair and kind person, worthy of real respect. This type of awareness of a moral demand is also God-given, arising from our God-given drive to reach our created potential.

Unbelieving moral philosophy has tended to isolate and absolutize these different ways of encountering the God-given moral law because there is usually not a significant awareness of the unity within complexity of God's general revelation, which is the source of much moral thinking and acting. This tendency to absolutize one dimension of our encounter with the moral law given in creation gives rise to the range of competing moral philosophies, many of which seek to explain all of moral experience in light of one dimension of moral experience. Most secular moral philosophies are reductionistic in the sense of reducing our perception of moral experience and moral obligation, because each moral philosophy tends to isolate and absolutize one part of moral experience. If we really believe that we live in God's created world through which he is continually speaking his moral law, we can easily begin to see that there is a deep unity and complementarity within these different ways of encountering his law in creation. Many believers do this without a second thought; perhaps only those who have read secular moral philosophy are aware that this is happening all the time within believing circles.

When we attempt to bring biblically informed moral principles into the public square in our secular societies, we have the freedom to select which dimension of the general revelation of God's moral law we want to emphasize on that occasion. On some occasions, when speaking for an audience or class which is predominantly made up of people who are not yet Christians, I have emphasized our direct intuitive awareness of certain moral duties like mercy, faithfulness, or honesty. In these situations, I have sounded a little like a follower of intuitional deontological ethical theory, which absolutizes that way of encountering the moral law of God given in creation. On other occasions, when speaking for an audience or class that is comprised mostly of non-believers, I have chosen to emphasize what kind of person we become as a result of particular actions. In that situation, I have sounded a little like a virtue moral theorist or a follower of Aristotle, the ethical theory that absolutizes the question of how a series of actions turns us into a certain type of person. And on still other occasions, when speaking to a class of unbelievers, I have focused the attention of my students on the predictable negative or positive results, sometimes demonstrated by studies in the social sciences, that follow from certain practices; for example, I have talked about the significant negative consequences for human well-being that usually flow from divorce and cohabitation. In that situation, I sounded a lot like a follower of rule-utilitarian moral theory, the type of moral theory that wants to derive all moral knowledge from predictable consequences of our actions. As a Christian, I have the freedom to invite people to think about the different dimensions of God's general revelation of his moral law, and a person who only heard a few minutes from one of those lectures might have mistakenly thought, on different days, that I was a virtue moral theorist, an intuitional moral theorist, or a rule utilitarian moral theorist. But my goal has been only to bring my hearers into significant contact with one of the many complementary ways in which we encounter God's moral law revealed through creation. And this has been with the intention of being both a bearer of common grace and also to make God's special revelation and special grace more plausible for a particular audience.

IX. The Same Moral Law Which Restrains Sin Also Convicts of Sin and Points Our Neighbors to the Gospel.

I have argued that believers need to be servants of God's common grace by means of effectively promoting humane moral standards in the public square, moral standards which arise from the general revelation of God's law and are informed by the special revelation of God's law. This process has been occurring for many centuries, and believers should consciously adopt the promotion of Righteousness No. 1 as part of our contribution to our various cultures. We should be consciously looking for suitable opportunities to help our neighbors see that things like telling the truth, protecting human rights, and being loyal to one's spouse and family are truly right and proper and contribute to human well-being. As servants of God's common grace, we should attempt to promote the civil use of the law and encourage adherence to God's law in its civil use.

As we pursue this part of the calling God has given us, we should never forget that God's law always retains all three of its uses: God's law always (1) shows us our sin and need for salvation in Christ; (2) restrains our sin to enable civic righteousness; and (3) is a guide for the life of gratitude toward God for his gifts of creation and redemption. It may be that in a certain situation, one of the uses of God's law is prominent in our minds, but God's law is always engaging people in multiple ways. In our discussion of ethics in the public square, we are mostly thinking about civic righteousness as a result of the restraint of sin, the second use of God's moral law; in certain times and places, that should be the main topic of our discussion. But God's law is frequently used by God's Spirit to also accomplish the other purposes of the moral law. And one of these functions is showing people their sinfulness and their need for the gospel of Christ. In this manner, the representation of the general revelation of God's moral law in the public square can also serve a pre-evangelistic function, preparing the way for the gospel. Some examples may help; these examples come primarily from my personal experience, whether teaching philosophy and ethics in secular universities or speaking in government policy conferences. In several situations, I have given lectures or speeches that have emphasized moral principles that lead to a humane way of life, under the blessing of God's common grace, while at the same time I have hoped the Holy Spirit was also using my speeches or lectures to show my hearers their need for forgiveness by faith in our Savior.

In public university lectures, I have argued that governments should not legalize active euthanasia, because we can observe a repeated tendency in human history for people to kill other people while deceiving themselves to think they are doing a good thing while killing someone else. How can we have any certainty that active euthanasia is not a repetition of this old problem? An astute Christian observer of that lecture would probably notice that this was truly a lecture on public ethics, intended to promote civic righteousness in regard to a particular question, while at the same time that lecture would also tend to show human sinfulness: we are the sort of people who can easily kill others and deceive ourselves about our murderous potential. Whether or not I have mentioned Christ or have explicitly said that we are wrestling with God's law, this lecture would both promote a humane society and also show the need for the gospel. God's law restrains our sin, while it also shows our need for forgiveness.

When teaching university classes on ethics, I have sometimes given a lecture based on studies in the social sciences that show that cohabitation and divorce generally lead to a wide range of negative consequences for all of the people involved, including the children who are conceived in these unions. My mode of reasoning has been consciously rule-utilitarian, asking what rule, if widely observed, would predictably lead to better conse- quences for the people most directly influenced by that rule. I have sug- gested that even an intelligent atheist who is honestly concerned about hu- man well-being will follow the traditional Christian rules which require lifetime marriage and keeping sexuality within marriage. An astute Chris- tian observer of such lecture would notice that it really was a serious lec- ture designed to promote civic moral responsibility in one of the crucial areas of ethical consideration, using a method of moral reasoning em- ployed by some of the most highly regarded secular moral philosophers; but this lecture was also an apology for the Christian faith. This lecture would have promoted civic righteousness, regardless of the faith or beliefs of the hearers; but for many hearers, it would also expose an area of guilt and the need for forgiveness, while making the biblical message more plausible. The moral law always tends to restrain sin as a means of com- mon grace, while also showing our sin and need for forgiveness in Christ.

In the speech mentioned above on family values for government policy makers, I had chosen to use the language and terminology of a direct intui- tive awareness of moral duties that should shape family values in all sec- tors of life. I decided to use this method of reasoning and presentation be- cause I thought it was suitable to the situation. My intention was to strengthen the awareness of certain parts of God's moral law in a manner that be used by God's common grace to restrain sin and promote healthy family life; but I was very conscious that God's law always has all of its functions, including guiding believers and showing our sin and need for salvation. It is highly probable that many of my hearers had a history of serious disloyalty to a spouse and children, leading to an awareness of guilt, which is a step toward seeing their need for Christ. My hope is that this lecture had a pre-evangelistic function in the sense of making a few people aware of their need for the gospel if they would have the opportuni- ty to hear the good news of Christ in the following days or months. God's law, even when presented in a very partial manner, retains all of its im- portant functions, restraining sin as a means of God's common grace, showing our need for forgiveness and special grace in Christ, and giving direction for the life of gratitude in response to God's special and common grace.

X. Comments

Jesus calls his followers to be in the world but not of the world. We are sent into the world as people who continually hear and carry his Word to a needy world. This does not only mean evangelism and seeking converts to Christ as servants of God's special grace; this also requires us to be servants of common grace, which is partly mediated through the civic use of God's moral law. Therefore, we need to learn how to become people who can communicate all or part of God's moral law into our various cultures in suitable ways. Believers have made truly massive contributions in this area for at least 2000 years, and contributing an awareness of God's law to our cultures needs to become an organic part of our understanding of the mission of the Body of Christ in the world. The right words from believers in their positions around the world can play a significant role in what billions of people decide to do. One set of words leads people to imitate Adolph Hitler; another set of words leads people to partly imitate Mother Teresa, even if they do not fully accept her faith. And those words that communicate the moral law which would restrain sin and promote civic righteousness will also tend to point out our sin and our need for Christ. Therefore, bringing biblical principles into the public square also contributes to the pre-evangelistic work of the Body of Christ.

About the Author

Biography

Thomas K. Johnson received his Ph.D. in ethics and philosophical theology from the University of Iowa (USA, 1987) after a research fellowship at Eberhard-Karls Universität (Tübingen, Germany). He received a Master of Divinity (*Magna Cum Laude*) from Covenant Theological Seminary (St. Louis, USA, 1981), and a BA from Hope College (Michigan, USA, 1977).

After serving as a church planter in the Presbyterian Church in America, he became a visiting professor of philosophy at the European Humanities University (EHU) in Minsk, Belarus, 1994–1996. (EHU is a dissident, anti-Communist university, forced into exile by the Belarusian dictator in 2004.)

Since 1996 Johnson and his wife have lived in Prague, where he taught philosophy at Anglo-American University (four years) and at Charles University (eight years). From 2004 to 2013 he was director of the Comenius Institute in Prague, which works to develop Czech Christian academic spokespeople. He began teaching apologetics, ethics, and theology for Martin Bucer Seminary in 2003 and has taught theology and philosophy in eleven universities or theological schools in nine countries.

Johnson is presently Vice President for Research, Martin Bucer European School of Theology and Research Institutes; Special Advisor to the International Institute for Religious Freedom (WEA); Professor of Philosophy, Global Scholars; ordained minister, Presbyterian Church in America; and Senior Advisor to the Theological Commission of the World Evangelical Alliance. In March, 2016, he was appointed Religious Freedom Ambassador to the Vatican, representing the World Evangelical Alliance and its 600 million members.

His wife, Leslie P. Johnson, was Director of the Christian International School of Prague, 2004-2015. She is currently an educational consultant affiliated with the Association of Christian Schools International. They have three married children and several grandchildren.

Publications by Dr. Johnson; for most of these materials you can click on the titles to read or download the texts. If you are reading in a printed version, a simple internet search should lead you to most of these titles.

Publications by Thomas K. Johnson which are readily available online, in libraries, or from the publisher:[99]

1. Books

Natural Law Ethics: An Evangelical Proposal, volume 6 in the Christian Philosophy Today series (Bonn: VKW, 2005).

What Difference Does the Trinity Make? A Complete Faith, Life, and Worldview, volume 7 in the Global Issues Series of the World Evangelical Alliance (Bonn: VKW, 2009).

The First Step in Missions Training: How Our Neighbors Are Wrestling with God's General Revelation, volume 1 in the World of Theology series published by the Theological Commission of the World Evangelical Alliance (Bonn: VKW, 2014).

Christian Ethics in Secular Cultures, volume 2 in the World of Theology series published by the Theological Commission of the World Evangelical Alliance (Bonn: VKW, 2014).

Human Rights: A Christian Primer, second edition, volume 1 in the Global Issues Series of the World Evangelical Alliance (Bonn: VKW, 2016).

Creation Care and Loving our Neighbors, with Thomas Schirrmacher, volume 17 in the Global Issues Series of the World Evangelical Alliance (Bonn: VKW, 2016).

Global Declarations on Freedom of Religion or Belief and Human Rights, selected and edited by Thomas K. Johnson with Thomas Schirrmacher and Christof Sauer, volume 18 in the Global Issues Series of the World Evangelical Alliance (Bonn: VKW, 2017).

Two of the book series of the World Evangelical Alliance in which Dr. Johnson is an editor, the *World of Theology* series published by the Theological Commission and the *Global Issues* series published by the International Institute for Religious Freedom, are available as free downloads here.

2. WEA Statements

The Bad Urach Call: Toward understanding suffering, persecution, and martyrdom for the global church in mission, 2010. This is a call to action ad-

---

[99] Several people have very kindly given their time and energy to assist with this publishing program. These include Ruth Baldwin, Dr. Johnson's primary editing assistant, along with John Colley, Russ Johnson, Patricia Foster, Anke Damson, and Bob Hussey.

dressed to the global evangelical movement which summarizes the larger Bad Urach Statement.

"Xenophobia, Hospitality, and the Refugee Crisis in Europe," September, 2015.

Dr. Johnson was the primary author of Efraim Tendero's speech on "The Gospel and Religious Extremism," March, 2016.

3. Booklets and essays on the WEA website

Adam and Eve, Who Are You? 2004.

Deceptive Philosophy, 2004.

Human Rights and Christian Ethics, 2005.

Progress, Knowledge, and God, 2005.

Interpreting the Ten Commandments: A Study in Special Hermeneutics, 2005.

Sex, Marriage, and Science, 2005.

Paul's Intellectual Courage in the Face of Sophisticated Unbelief, 2006.

Christ and Culture, 2007.

Biblical Principles in the Public Square: Theological Foundations for Christian Civic Participation, 2008.

Foundational Political Values to Guide Governmental and Family Care of Children, 2008.

What Makes Sex So Special? 2009.

The Moral Crisis of the West, 2009.

The Spirit of the Protestant Work Ethic and the World Economic Crisis, 2009.

Human Rights and the Human Quest, 2009.

Rights, Religions, and Ideologies, 2009.

Law and Gospel: The Hermeneutical/Homiletical Key to Reformation Theology and Ethics, 2009.

Triple Knowledge and the Reformation Faith, 2009.

"Thinking Twice about the Minaret Ban in Switzerland," 2009.

"Why Evangelicals Need a Code of Ethics for Missions," with Thomas Schirrmacher, 2010.

Translated, edited, and expanded "Defection from Islam: A Disturbing Human Rights Dilemma" by Christine Schirrmacher, 2010.

Translated and edited "Islamic Human Rights Declarations and Their Critics" by Christine Schirrmacher, 2011.

"In Context: Christian Witness in a Multi-Religious World: Recommendations for Conduct," 2011.

Sabbath, Work, and the Quest for Meaning, 2011.

Education and the Human Quest: The Correlation of Existence and History, 2011.

"May Christians Go to Court?" With Thomas Schirrmacher, 2011.

Dutch Reformed Philosophy in North America: Three Varieties in the Late Twentieth Century, 2012.

The Protester, the Dissident, and the Christian, 2012.

4. Other booklets and essays available online

"That Which Is Noteworthy and That Which Is Astonishing in the Global Charter of Conscience," IJRF 5:1, 2012, 7-9.

"Religious Freedom and the Twofold Work of God in the World," IJRF 6:1/2 2013, 17-24.

"Dualisms, Dualities, and Creation Care," with Thomas Schirrmacher, World Reformed Fellowship, November, 2013.

Dialogue with Kierkegaard in Protestant Theology: Donald Bloesch, Francis Schaeffer, and Helmut Thielicke, MBS Text 175, 2013.

The Trinity in the Bible and Selected Creeds of the Church, MBS Text 179, 2013.

Foreword entitled "The Holistic Mission of William Carey," in *William Carey: Theologian – Linguist – Social Reformer,* edited by Thomas Schirrmacher, volume 4 in the World of Theology Series of the WEA Theological Commission, 2013.

"The Crisis of Modernity and the Task of Moral Philosophy," World Reformed Fellowship, April, 2014.

"Faith and Reason Active in Love: The Theology of Creation Care," with Thomas Schirrmacher, World Reformed Fellowship, May, 2014.

"The Church's Complex Relationship with the Idea of Wealth and Need," a speech given at the Pontifical Academy of Social Sciences, the Vatican, June, 2014, published by the World Reformed Fellowship.

"Why Is Religious Extremism So Attractive? Life Together and the Search for Meaning," IJRF, vol. 7 1/2, 2014, 9-12.

Family/Sexual Chaos and the Evangelical Faith, November, 2014, a booklet prepared on behalf of the Theological Commission of the World Evangelical Alliance and submitted to the Vatican Synod on the Family, published by the World Reformed Fellowship.

"Lessons from Paris 2015: Clash of Civilizations or Battling Nihilisms?" published by the World Reformed Fellowship, January, 2015.

Foreword entitled, "The Moral Structure of the Condemnation of Slavery in Amos," in *The Humanisation of Slavery in the Old Testament*, edited by Thomas Schirrmacher, volume 8 in the World of Theology Series of the WEA Theological Commission, 2015.

"Religious Terrorism, Brussels, and the Search for Meaning," *Evangelical Focus,* 29 March, 2016.

"Addressing the Scars on the Face of Christendom," World Reformed Fellowship, September 23, 2016.

Learning to Love the Persecuted Church, MBS Text 186, 2016.

Why is the Virgin Birth so Important? MBS Text 187, 2017.

Poverty and Chastity in Reformed Ethics MBS Text 188, 2017.

With Thomas Schirrmacher, "Let the Reformation Continue!" World Reformed Fellowship, March 26, 2017.

5. Books edited by Dr. Johnson

Edited and wrote a foreword entitled "The Bible and Global Social Problems," Thomas Schirrmacher, *Racism, With an Essay by Richard Howell on Caste in India,* the WEA Global Issues Series, volume 8, 2011.

Edited and wrote a foreword entitled "The Father of Modern Education," Jan Habl, *Lessons in Humanity: From the Life and Work of Jan Amos Komensky,* 2011, on the WEA CD zip file found at http://www.bucer.de/ressourcen/wea-cd.html.

Christine Schirrmacher, *The Sharia: Law and Order in Islam,* the WEA Global Issues Series, volume 10, 2013.

Thomas Schirrmacher, *Human Trafficking: The Return to Slavery,* the WEA Global Issues Series, volume 12, 2013.

Edited and wrote a foreword entitled "Ethics for Christians in the World," Thomas Schirrmacher, *Leadership and Ethical Responsibility: The Three Aspect of Every Decision,* the WEA Global Issues Series, volume 13, 2013.

Thomas Schirrmacher, *Fundamentalism: When Religion Becomes Dangerous,* the WEA Global Issues Series, volume 14, 2013.

Thomas Schirrmacher, *Advocate of Love: Martin Bucer as Theologian and Pastor,* volume 5 in the World of Theology Series, 2013.

Thomas Schirrmacher, *Culture of Shame/Culture of Guilt,* volume 6 in the World of Theology Series, 2013.

Edited and revised Thomas Schirrmacher, *The Koran and the Bible,* volume 7 in the World of Theology Series, 2013.

Ken Gnanakan, *Responsible Stewardship of God's Creation,* the WEA Global Issues Series, volume 11, 2014.

Edited and wrote a foreword entitled "The Holocaust and German Thought on Human Rights," Thomas Schirrmacher, *Human Rights: Promise and Reality,* the WEA Global Issues Series, volume 15, 2014.

Edited and wrote a foreword for Jan Habl, *Teaching and Learning Through Story: Comenius' Labyrinth and the Educational Potential of Narrative Allegory,* 2014, on the WEA CD zip file found at http://www.bucer.de/ressourcen/wea-cd.html.

Christine Schirrmacher, *Political Islam: When Faith Turns Out to Be Politics*, the WEA Global Issues Series, volume 16, 2016. http://www.bucer.org/uploads/tx_org/WEA_GIS_16_Christine_Schirrmacher_-_Political_Islam.pdf.

World Evangelical Alliance

World Evangelical Alliance is a global ministry working with local churches around the world to join in common concern to live and proclaim the Good News of Jesus in their communities. WEA is a network of churches in 129 nations that have each formed an evangelical alliance and over 100 international organizations joining together to give a worldwide identity, voice and platform to more than 600 million evangelical Christians. Seeking holiness, justice and renewal at every level of society – individual, family, community and culture, God is glorified and the nations of the earth are forever transformed.

Christians from ten countries met in London in 1846 for the purpose of launching, in their own words, "a new thing in church history, a definite organization for the expression of unity amongst Christian individuals belonging to different churches." This was the beginning of a vision that was fulfilled in 1951 when believers from 21 countries officially formed the World Evangelical Fellowship. Today, 150 years after the London gathering, WEA is a dynamic global structure for unity and action that embraces 600 million evangelicals in 129 countries. It is a unity based on the historic Christian faith expressed in the evangelical tradition. And it looks to the future with vision to accomplish God's purposes in discipling the nations for Jesus Christ.

Commissions:

- Theology
- Missions
- Religious Liberty

- Women's Concerns
- Youth
- Information Technology

Initiatives and Activities

- Ambassador for Human Rights
- Ambassador for Refugees
- Creation Care Task Force
- Global Generosity Network
- International Institute for Religious Freedom

- International Institute for Islamic Studies
- Leadership Institute
- Micah Challenge
- Global Human Trafficking Task Force
- Peace and Reconciliation Initiative
- UN-Team

Church Street Station
P.O. Box 3402
New York, NY 10008-3402
Phone +[1] 212 233 3046
Fax +[1] 646-957-9218
www.worldea.org

Giving Hands

GIVING HANDS GERMANY (GH) was established in 1995 and is officially recognized as a nonprofit foreign aid organization. It is an international operating charity that – up to now – has been supporting projects in about 40 countries on four continents. In particular we care for orphans and street children. Our major focus is on Africa and Central America. GIVING HANDS always mainly provides assistance for self-help and furthers human rights thinking.

The charity itself is not bound to any church, but on the spot we are co-operating with churches of all denominations. Naturally we also cooperate with other charities as well as governmental organizations to provide assistance as effective as possible under the given circumstances.

The work of GIVING HANDS GERMANY is controlled by a supervisory board. Members of this board are Manfred Feldmann, Colonel V. Doner and Kathleen McCall. Dr. Christine Schirrmacher is registered as legal manager of GIVING HANDS at the local district court. The local office and work of the charity are coordinated by Rev. Horst J. Kreie as executive manager. Dr. theol. Thomas Schirrmacher serves as a special consultant for all projects.

Thanks to our international contacts companies and organizations from many countries time and again provide containers with gifts in kind which we send to the different destinations where these goods help to satisfy elementary needs. This statutory purpose is put into practice by granting nutrition, clothing, education, construction and maintenance of training centers at home and abroad, construction of wells and operation of water treatment systems, guidance for self-help and transportation of goods and gifts to areas and countries where needy people live.

GIVING HANDS has a publishing arm under the leadership of Titus Vogt, that publishes human rights and other books in English, Spanish, Swahili and other languages.

These aims are aspired to the glory of the Lord according to the basic Christian principles put down in the Holy Bible.

Baumschulallee 3a • D-53115 Bonn • Germany
Phone: +49 / 228 / 695531 • Fax +49 / 228 / 695532
www.gebende-haende.de • info@gebende-haende.de

Martin Bucer Seminary

Faithful to biblical truth
Cooperating with the Evangelical Alliance
Reformed

Solid training for the Kingdom of God

- Alternative theological education
- Study while serving a church or working another job
- Enables students to remain in their own churches
- Encourages independent thinking
- Learning from the growth of the universal church.

Academic

- For the Bachelor's degree: 180 Bologna-Credits
- For the Master's degree: 120 additional Credits
- Both old and new teaching methods: All day seminars, independent study, term papers, etc.

Our Orientation:

- Complete trust in the reliability of the Bible
- Building on reformation theology
- Based on the confession of the German Evangelical Alliance
- Open for innovations in the Kingdom of God

Our Emphasis:

- The Bible
- Ethics and Basic Theology
- Missions
- The Church

Our Style:

- Innovative
- Relevant to society
- International
- Research oriented
- Interdisciplinary

Structure

- 15 study centers in 7 countries with local partners
- 5 research institutes
- President: Prof. Dr. Thomas Schirrmacher
  Vice President: Prof. Dr. Thomas K. Johnson
- Deans: Thomas Kinker, Th.D.;
  Titus Vogt, lic. theol., Carsten Friedrich, M.Th.

Missions through research

- Institute for Religious Freedom
- Institute for Islamic Studies
- Institute for Life and Family Studies
- Institute for Crisis, Dying, and Grief
  Counseling
- Institute for Pastoral Care

www.bucer.eu • info@bucer.eu

Berlin | Bielefeld | Bonn | Chemnitz | Hamburg | Munich | Pforzheim
Innsbruck | Istanbul | Izmir | Linz | Prague | São Paulo | Tirana | Zurich

Printed in the USA
CPSIA information can be obtained
at www.ICGtesting.com
LVHW010251121223
766264LV00049B/1910